Success to IELTS

TIPS AND TECHNIQUES

Dr. ROMA

BJMC, M.A., PH.D. (ENGLISH)
EX-LECTURER KHALSA COLLEGE &
GURU NANAK DEV UNIVERSITY
(Dept. of English)

INDIA • SINGAPORE • MALAYSIA

Notion Press

Old No. 38, New No. 6
McNichols Road, Chetpet
Chennai - 600 031

First Published by Notion Press 2019
Copyright © Dr. Roma 2019
All Rights Reserved.

ISBN 978-1-68466-693-5

The content of this book has been designed after a comprehensive research from various forums of the net and based on the experience of the author, the best has been extracted out of it. Reference links have been provided below for further guidance and assistance for the students.

http://sckool.org/ielts-reading-test.html?page=9

https://ielts-up.com/reading/academic-reading-sample-8.1.html

https://ielts-mentor.com/reading-sample/gt-reading/3135-renting-accommodation-in-stonington-and-blossom-child-care

https://www.ielts-mentor.com/reading-sample/gt-reading/3185-shoe-world-and-cd-directory0

CONTENTS

READING TEST

FORMAT

- ➤ This module lasts for an hour (60 minutes).

- ➤ There is no extra time given to transfer the answers.

- ➤ This module is different for both academic and general training students.

- ➤ Reading booklet contains three sections with 40 questions in all.

MARKING

- ➤ Each question is worth one mark for both the modules.

- ➤ Spelling is extremely important. Check your spellings once before transferring the question to the main answer booklet.

- ➤ Grammar also carries marks. For instance, if the answer requires you to convert singular into plural or change the tense, then you have to do it or else marks will be deducted.

- ➤ Write answer with clear handwriting, or else you might lose marks.

- ➤ A hyphenated word (e.g. absent-minded) counts as one word.

TIPS

- ➤ Have a quick look at the type of questions asked, you'll know what you will be expecting in the reading passages.

- ➤ Don't try to understand every word you stumble upon. The reading is meant to be read, not understood.

- Learn the trick of skimming and scanning. In this way, you will save a lot of time.

- Do not spend more than 15–20 minutes on each passage and try to write the answers on the answer sheet.

- Read the instructions for the questions very carefully. Always look for the word count in answers.

- Don't panic. Stay calm and relaxed.

- Don't stress too much over one question if you don't know the answer. Make a guess and move on to the next question.

Solved Example Academic

You should spend about 20 minutes on Questions 1–14, which are based on Reading Passage 1 below.

This Is Very Much the Story of a Story

The outline of the tale has been told before. It can be found in Edward Miller's history of the British Museum, <u>Arundell Esdaile's book on the British Museum Library</u>, rather more chattily, in <u>Edward Edwards's Lives of the founders of the Museum</u>, and most recently, and its first excursion this century outside the literature of the Museum, <u>in Christopher Hibbert's new biography of George III.</u> (**1**-*three books of different publications have been mentioned*)

The December 1850 issue of the Quarterly Review contains a long article reviewing a number of official reports into the functioning of the British Museum (including incidentally a review of the House of Commons Select Committee report of 1836, fifteen years earlier: it is never too late to review a good report. <u>Although anonymous</u> (**2**-*it was anonymous at the time*), <u>it was written by Richard Ford</u> (**3**-*writer's name is given*), <u>probably best remembered today as the author of Murray's Handbook for travellers in Spain.</u> (**5**-*Murray was only in the name of the book not the writer, writer was Richard Ford*)

The review contains much that is entertaining and amusing, and I must say it can be recommended today to anyone concerned with organising Library services, but for our purposes the bit that matters is the allegation that, among other things, <u>George IV had been considering selling George III's library to the Tsar of Russia,</u>(**4**) until the British government intervened and arranged for its transfer instead to the British Museum.

This story was picked up during 1851 by a number of contributors to Notes & Queries, where various mischievous observations about what happened and who was involved were made. These comments revolved chiefly round the suggestion that the <u>King's Library</u> (7) was not the <u>munificent gift</u> (8) to the nation that it was claimed to be, but that the government had in effect <u>had to buy the Library</u>, (6-*the amount is not mentioned*) either directly by purchase, or indirectly by agreeing to treat the King's requests for money more sympathetically than hitherto.

In August 1851, however, came a communication to Notes & Queries of a different kind from the previous notes, which are rather gossipier in nature. It is signed "C." He writes: "I have delayed contradicting the stories tol8 about the King's Library in the Quarterly Review of last December... I am sorry to say still more gravely and circumstantially reproduced by the Editor of Notes & Queries. I have delayed, I say, until I was enabled to satisfy myself more completely as to one of the allegations in your Note."

"C." goes on: "I can now venture to assure you that the whole story of the projected sale to Russia is <u>absolutely unfounded</u>" (9). He then goes on to sketch in background about George IV's wish to dispose of the Library and the government's success in getting it to the British Museum.

"C." then objects in particular to the suggestion, made by the Notes & Queries editor rather than in the Quarterly, that Princess Lieven, the well-known socialite and friend of George IV's, whose husband was Russian ambassador in London at the time, had been <u>involved in the plan</u> (10-*the third word of this paragraph says "objects," which means he denied*). He explains that Princess Lieven was adamant that she had known of no such proposal, and therefore that that was that.

But that was not that. The December issue of Notes & Queries includes a short note, signed "Griffin," arguing that while Princess Lieven may claim to have known nothing, <u>it did not mean that there had not been talk about a Russian purchase.</u> (11) "Griffin" <u>also suggests that one of the King's motives for getting rid of the Library was to sort out problems arising from George Ill's Will</u> (12) (a suggestion, as has been pointed out before, that is incidentally supported by an entry from early 1823 in the journal of Charles Greville).

This provoked "C." to return to the matter in early 1852, when he argued that it was inconceivable that Princess Lieven would not have known that such a thing was in the air, given her court and social connections.

In other words, the Russian connection is just idle speculation.

An interesting aspect of all this is that the initial stirring and rumour-mongering was all to do with money: was the library, or was it not, paid for? It is the intervention of "C." and his fervent denials that bring the Russians into prominence.

The identity of "C." is obscure (**13**-*obscure means unsure*). Arundell Esdaile identifies him as John Wilson Croker, the veteran politician (**14**) and essayist. This seems to me unlikely: Croker was certainly involved in public affairs in the 1820's, but he was also a major contributor, a sort of editorial advisor, to the Quarterly Review, where the original offending article appeared. Indeed, he wrote his own piece for it on the Museum in the December 1852 issue, without referring at all to the King's Library stories, and referring to Richard Ford's article in respectful not to say glowing terms. A footnote to his article, however, states that the Quarterly expected to publish an authoritative account of the King's Library business in the future: it never did.

Questions 1–6

Do the statements below agree with the information in Reading Passage 1?

In Boxes 1–6, write:

YES if the statement agrees with the information in the passage

NO if the statement contradicts the information in the passage

NOT GIVEN if there is no information about the statement in the passage

Example: The outline of the tale has been told before.

Answer: Yes.

1. The story that the writer is telling has only ever been carried in publications relating to the British Museum.

2. When published, the review of several reports on the workings of the British Museum in the Quarterly Review was anonymous.

3. The writer claims that it was Richard Ford who wrote the review of several reports on the workings of the British Museum in the Quarterly Review.

4. Richard Ford alleged that George III was planning to sell his father's, i.e. George III's, library to the Tsar of Russia.

5. Murray wrote the Handbook for travellers to Spain.

6. The British Government bought George IV's father's library for a very large sum of money.

Questions 7–10

Complete the sentences below. Use NO MORE THAN FOUR WORDS from the passage to complete each blank space.

Write your answers in Boxes 7–10 on your answer sheet.

7. George IV's father's collection of books is known as the
   _____.

8. Doubting that the collection was given to the nation, some commentators said it was not a _____.

9. "C." says that the story about the sale of the books to Russia was
   _____.

10. According to "C.," Princess Lieven was not _____.

Questions 11–14

Choose the appropriate letters A-D and write them in Boxes 11–14 on your answer sheet.

11. 'Griffin' argued that the connection with Russia…

   A. could not be trusted.

   B. was genuine.

   C. was possible.

   D. was worth examining.

12. Charles Greville…

   A. does not corroborate Griffin's suggestion that the sale of the Library was connected with George III's Will.

   B. partially supports Griffin's suggestion that the sale of the Library was connected with George III's Will.

   C. corroborates Griffin's suggestion that the sale of the Library was connected with George III's Will.

   D. was Prime Minister in the early 1820s.

13. Which of the following is true according to the text?

    A. The identity of "C." is obvious

    B. The identity of "C." is not clear

    C. The identity of "C." is Arundell Esdaile

    D. The identity of "C." is John Wilson Croker

14. Croker…

    A. had been a politician for a long time

    B. was an editor

    C. was someone who advised politicians

    D. was a minor contributor to Notes & Queries

Answers

1. NO	**8.** MUNIFICENT GIFT
2. YES	**9.** ABSOLUTELY UNFOUNDED
3. YES	**10.** INVOLVED IN THE PLAN
4. YES	**11.** C
5. NO	**12.** C
6. NOT GIVEN	**13.** B
7. KING'S LIBRARY	**14.** A

READING PASSAGE 2

You should spend about 20 minutes on Questions 15–27, which are based on Reading Passage 2 below.

De Profundis Clamavi

A. But not too loud! According to the Royal National Institute for Deaf People, there has been a threefold increase in hearing loss and, in the future, deafness will become an epidemic. It is hardly surprising that new research shows complaints about noise, in particular loud music and barking dogs, are on the increase. So dire has the situation become that the National Society for Clean Air and the Environment was even moved to designate 7 June 2000 as Noise Action Day.

B. There are so many different sources of noise competing for people's attention. Travelling on a train as it saunters gently through the countryside was once a civilised and enjoyable experience. That delight has all but disappeared. Because we have to reach our destination more quickly, the train hurtles at breakneck speed along tracks not designer to carry carriages at such high velocity. <u>The train is noisier. And so are the occupants</u> (**15**-*since they are talking about the noisy travellers in the train*). They have to compete with the din of the train; and the conversations of them fellow travellers. And then there are the ubiquitous headphones (one set if you're lucky); not to mention that bane of all travellers, the mobile phone-not one's own, of course, because one has switched it off. The noise sensitive, a growing minority group, are hit by a double whammy here: the phone going off and the person answering in a loud voice, because they cannot believe the other person can hear. And let US not forget computer games making horrid noises given by parents to keep them children quiet! It is, however, gratifying to see that some train companies request people to keep the volume of them headphones down. It still strikes one as strange that people have to be reminded to do this. Like no-smoking carriages <u>we should have more no-noise carriages</u> (**22**-*solution to noisy train problem*): mobile-free, headphone-free, computer-free zones!

14

C. And the answer? Stay at home? No, not really. <u>The neighbours do DIY: if you are lucky between 9 a.m. and 7 p.m., and, if you are not, 24 hours a day.</u> (**16**-*they talk about the noises neighbours make*). They play loud music, sing, play the piano, rip up their carpets; they jump up and down on bare floorboards to annoy you further. They have loud parties to irritate you and cats, dogs and children that jump onto bare wooden floors and make your heart stop. And, because they want to hear the music in other parts of them flat they pump up the volume, so that you can feel the noise as well as hear it. And if you are very fortunate, they attach the stereo to the walls above your settee, so that you can vibrate as well. Even if you live in a semi-detached or detached property, they will still get you.

D. <u>People escape to the countryside and return to the urban environment.</u> (**17**-*here, it is said that, although people escape or move to different areas, the noise persists, and thus it has the same environment of noise*). They cannot tolerate the noise – the tractors, the cars and the motorbikes ripping the air apart as they career along country roads. Then there are the country dirt-track rallies that destroy the tranquillity of country week-ends and holidays. And we mustn't forget die birds! Believe me, the dawn chorus is something to contend with. <u>So, when you go to the countryside, make sure you take your industrial ear-muffs with you!</u> (**26**-*the solution to the noise in the countryside*).

E. <u>A quiet evening at the cinema, perhaps, or a restaurant? The former will have the latest all-round stereophonic eardrum-bursting sound system, with which they will try to deafen you.</u> (**18**-*the entertaining areas also have high-pitched noise. Note that the paragraph does not talk about the restaurants alone, so option (ix) is incorrect*). Film soundtracks register an average of 82 decibels with the climax of some films hitting as high as 120! And, in the restaurant, you will be waited on by waiters who have been taking them employers to court, because the noise in their working environment is way above the legal limits. Normal conversation registers at 60 decibels. But noise levels of up to 90 are frequent in today's restaurants. The danger level is considered to be any noise above 85 decibels! What is it doing to your eardrums then? Shopping is also out, because stereophonic sound systems have landed there, too.

F. Recently the law in the United Kingdom has been changed vis-à-vis noise, with stiffer penalties: (**19**-*the laws regarding the noise are talked about here*) fines, confiscation of stereo equipment and eviction for serious offences. Noise curfews could also be imposed in residential areas by enforcing restrictions on noise levels after certain times in the evenings. Tighter legislation is a step in the right direction. But there is no one solution to the problem, least of all recourse to the law; in fact, in some well-publicised cases, the legal and bureaucratic process has been unbearable enough to drive people to suicide.

G. The situation needs to be addressed from a variety of different angles simultaneously. There are practical solutions like using building materials in flats and houses that absorb sound: (**19**-*practical solutions are discussed*) sound-proofing material is already used in recording studios and, (**25**-*the solution for households*) whilst it is far from cheap to install, with research and mass sales, prices will come down. Designers have begun to realise that there is a place for soft furnishings in restaurants, like carpets, soft wall-coverings and cushions. (**24**-*solution for restaurants*). As well as creating a relaxing ambiance, they absorb the noise.

H. Informal solutions like mediation are also frequently more effective than legislation. And the answer may partly be found in the wider social context. (**21**-*the paragraph talks about the solutions society can provide*). The issue is surely one of public awareness and of politeness, of respect for neighbours, of good manners, and also of citizenship; in effect, how individuals operate within a society and relate to each other. And, perhaps, we need to be taught once again to tolerate silence.

Questions 15–21

Reading Passage 2 has 8 paragraphs (A–H). Choose the most suitable heading for each paragraph from the list of headings below. Write the appropriate numbers (i–xiii) in Boxes 15–21 on your answer sheet.

One of the headings has been done for you as an example.

NB. There are more headings than paragraphs, so you will not use all of them.

15. Paragraph B

16. Paragraph C

17. Paragraph D

18. Paragraph E

19. Paragraph F

20. Paragraph G

21. Paragraph H

List of Headings

  i. Social solutions

 ii. The law backs noise

iii. Some practical solutions

 iv. The beautiful countryside

  v. Noise from mobiles

 vi. Neighbour noise

vii. Noisy travellers

viii. Noise to entertain you

 ix. Noisy restaurants

  x. The law and noise

 xi. Rural peace shattered

xii. A quite evening at the restaurant

xiii. Noise on the increase

Questions 22–27

The passage contains a number of solutions for particular areas where noise is a problem. Match the solutions (A–L) to the problem areas (22–27). If no solution is given, choose A as the answer. Write the appropriate letters (A–L) in Boxes 22–27 on your answer sheet.

NB. There are more solutions (A–L) than sentences, so you will not need to use them all. Except for A, you may use each solution once only.

22. Trains

23. Cinemas

24. Restaurants

25. Homes

26. Living in a rural setting

27. Shops

List of Solutions

G. Music should be turned down.

H. The noise laws should be relaxed.

I. Shops should have restricted opening hours.

J. Trains should be sound-proofed.

K. More noise-free carriages should be introduced on trains.

L. Visitors should carry industrial earmuffs.

Answers

15. VII	22. K
16. VI	23. A
17. XI	24. D
18. VIII	25. F
19. X	26. L
20. III	27. A
21. I	

READING PASSAGE 3

You should spend about 20 minutes on Questions 28–40, which are based on Reading Passage 3 below.

Classical and Modern

In the United Kingdom at university level, the decline in the study of Latin and Greek, the classics, has been reversed. As a result of renewed interest in reading classical literature and history, <u>more and more students are enrolling on classical studies courses.</u> (**28**-*not less but more students are getting admitted*). The purists may deplore this development– (**29**-classists are condemning (deplore) this situation, not welcoming it) 'it is yet another example of the 'dumbing down' of tertiary education with students studying classical literature and history in English rather than the original languages.' And, I must admit, they do have a point. <u>But the situation is surely not as dire as the ultimate demise of classics as an intellectual discipline.</u> (**30**-*not agreeing*).

A classical education is a <u>boon</u> (**32**) and should be encouraged. But, before looking at the advantages of studying the classics, which appear, incidentally, more indirect and less tangible than other disciplines, let US examine the criticisms that are often levelled against studying Latin and Greek.

The Decline in the Teaching of Classics

The 60s with their trendy ideas in education are blamed for the steady decline in studying the classics. But the rot had set in much earlier, when Latin and Greek were no longer required for university entrance. With the introduction of the National Curriculum in secondary schools came the biggest blow. Schools came under pressure to devote more time to core subjects like English, mathematics, the sciences, history and geography. This left scant room for the more 'peripheral' subject area$ like the classics. There was a further squeeze with the rush into teaching IT and computing skills. As schools could no longer choose what they wanted to teach, so subjects like the classics were further <u>marginalised.</u> (**33**) Take Latin. In 1997, 11,694 pupils took Latin GCSE, while, in 1988, the number was 17,000. Comprehensive schools now supply 40% fewer

Latin candidates, whereas grammar schools have seen a 20% decline. Latin candidates from Independent schools have fallen by only 5%. As a consequence, classics has been relegated to the 'better' grammar or comprehensive schools, and the minor and great public schools. Only one third of Latin GCSE entries come from the state sector. It can, therefore, be of no surprise to anyone when the pursuit of a classical education is attacked as <u>elitist.</u> **(34)**

Tainted by this misconception, the classics are then further <u>damned</u> **(35)** as being <u>irrelevant</u> **(36)** in the modem world. Having been pushed into such a tight comer, it is difficult to fight free. A classical education is so unlike, say, business studies or accountancy where young people can go directly into a profession and find a job easily. For classicists, this is not an option. Other than teaching, there is no specific <u>professional</u> **(37)** route after leaving university. And, with the pressure in the present climate to have a job, it is less easy than previously for young people to resist the pressure from the world outside academia, and from their families, to study something else that will make them money. The relevancy <u>argument</u> **(38)** is a hard nut to crack.

The Pertinence of a Classical Education

Latin and Greek have been damned as dead languages that offer US nothing. The response to this criticism is, in fact, straightforward. Most European languages are a development of the classical continuum. And so, having even a rudimentary knowledge prepares pupils for understanding other modem European languages. As for pertinence in the modem world, learning Latin and Greek are highly <u>relevant.</u> **(39)** The study of these languages, develops analytical skills that have, to a large extent, been <u>lost.</u> **(40)** They teach discipline and thinking and open up the whole of Western civilisation just as the discovery of the classical world did during the Renaissance.

Latin has also been called food for the brain. It gives students a grounding in the allusions in much of European literature and thought. Modem writers do not use these allusions themselves, first, because they do not know them, and, second, because their audience does not know them either. Sadly, most people no longer have the ability to interpret the allusions in art and the same has happened with the classics vis-à-vis literature.

The danger to Western and world culture is great if the classical tradition is lost. The spiral of decline is not just restricted to the United Kingdom. Other European countries face the same loss to their heritage. If we abandon the classics, we will not be able to interpret our past and to know where we have come from. A common refrain in modem society is the lack of thinking ability among even the best graduates. They enter work, perhaps as bright as any of their predecessors. But without the necessary skills they ran around trying to reinvent the wheel. As Ecclesiastes says: nihil novum sub sole est.

But help is at hand. Concerned by the fact that fewer and fewer teenagers have access to a range of foreign languages, the government is harnessing the power of the Internet to introduce a distance-learning programme, where pupils will study Latin and other minority languages at their own pace. Initially piloted in 60 schools from autumn 2000, the internet-based courses will enable pupils to access advice from specialists by e-mail.

Questions 28–31

Do the statements below agree with the information in Reading Passage 3?

In Boxes 28–31, write:

YES if the statement agrees with the information in the passage.

NO if the statement contradicts the information in the passage.

NOT GIVEN if there is no information about the statement in the passage.

Example: The decline in the study of Latin and Greek at university in the United Kingdom has been reversed.

Answer: Yes.

28. Fewer students are reading classical studies at university than before.

29. The purists welcome classical studies courses unreservedly.

30. The writer agrees fully with the purists' point of view.

31. A classical education is frowned upon in political circles.

Questions 32–40

Complete the text below, which is a summary of the writer's opinion on a classical education. Use One Word Only from the text to complete each blank space. Write your answers in Boxes 32–40 on your answer sheet.

You may use each word once only.

Example: Latin and Greek are known as the…

The writer considers a classical education to be a… (32)

Answer: classics.

He believes that, in secondary school, the teaching of classics has been … (33) by the introduction of the National Curriculum. This has further led to the studying of the classics being attacked as … (34). In addition, studying Latin and Greek is wrongly … (35) as being … (36), because classicists have no specific …(37) route to follow. As young people are pressurised to make money, the writer feels that the relevancy … (38) is difficult to counter.

In spite of the criticisms levelled at a classical education, the writer feels that learning Latin and Greek is highly… (39). And he fears that there is a danger that the classics as a discipline will be … (40). But help is at hand from a new Internet-based distance-learning programme being piloted in 60 schools from autumn 2000. The pilot study will allow pupils to study Latin at their own pace.

Answers

28. NO		35. DAMNED	
29. NO		36. IRRELEVANT	
30. NO		37. PROFESSIONAL	
31. NOT GIVEN		38. ARGUMENT	
32. BOON		39. RELEVANT/PERTINENT	
33. MARGINALISED		40. LOST	
34. ELITIST			

Hands-On

➤ **Example 1**

READING PASSAGE 1

Harsh Marks 'Put Pupils Off Languages'

A. Harsh and inconsistent marking is putting pupils in England off studying languages beyond age 14, a report says. The dawn of more rigorous GCSEs will further reduce interest in languages, research by the British Council and Education Development Trust suggests. It says a focus on maths and sciences, as well as a perception language are a hard option, is also de-motivating pupils and teachers.

B. Exam watchdog Ofqual said last year's languages results were "very stable." From September 2016, new GCSE and A-level modern language syllabuses will be taught in England, and new exams will be taken in the summer of 2018. The Language Trends Survey, in its 14th year of charting the state of language learning in England's schools, suggests these changes—particularly at A-level—will deter pupils from studying languages. It says: "The exam system is seen as one of the principal barriers to the successful development of language teaching." The comparative difficulty of exams in languages in relation to other subjects, and widely reported harsh and inconsistent marking, are deeply de-motivating for both pupils and teachers."

C. The report says the EBacc, where pupils have to study English, a language, maths, science and history or geography to GCSE, "appears to be having very little impact on the numbers of pupils taking languages post-16." Uptake after GCSE is found to be a particular concern, with some state schools suggesting the small numbers of students opting to take languages at A-level means the subject is becoming "financially unviable."

D. The proportion of the total cohort sitting a GCSE in a language dropped by one percentage point (to 48%) between 2014 and 2015, ending the rise in entries seen from 2012 onward, when the EBacc was brought in. Entries for each of the three main languages fell this year compared with 2014, French is down 6%, German is down 10% and Spanish is down 3%. Overall, entries for languages at A-level are at 94% of their 2002 level, and they declined by 3% between 2014 and 2015—French uptake declined by 1% and German by 2.5% while Spanish uptake rose by almost 15%.

E. The report does note some positive developments, particularly at the primary level, saying just over half of England's primary schools now have access to specialist expertise in the teaching of languages. But primary schools report finding it hard to fit languages into the curriculum time available and to recruit suitably qualified teaching staff. Teresa Tinsley, co-author of the report, said: "Languages are already one of the harder GCSEs, and teachers fear that with the new exams it will be even tougher for pupils to get a good grade." Combine this with the expectation that a wider range of pupils will be sitting the exam and it is not surprising that teachers feel embattled. "Improving their morale and confidence in the exam system is crucial if languages are to thrive in our schools."

F. A spokesman for the exam regulator, Ofqual, said: "We are committed to ensuring that all GCSEs, AS- and A-levels, including those in modern foreign languages, are sufficiently valid, produce fair and reliable results and have a positive impact on teaching and learning. "Last year's results in modern foreign languages were very stable, with only small changes in the proportions achieving each grade compared to the previous year. "We have looked into concerns that it is harder for students to achieve the highest grades in A level language. "We found this is because of the way the exams are designed, rather than the nature of the subject content. "We are keeping this under review and will be further publishing information shortly."

G. Referring to the new modern foreign language A-levels and GCSEs being taught from this September, the spokesman added: "Before we accredit a qualification, we check the exams will be designed to allow good differentiation – including that the best students will be able to achieve the highest grades – and whether they are properly based on the new subject content."

H. Mark Herbert, head of school's programmes at the British Council, said: "The country's current shortage of language skills is estimated to be costing the economy tens of billions in missed trade and business opportunities every year." "Parents, schools and businesses can all play their part in encouraging our young people to study languages at school and to ensure that language learning is given back the respect and prominence that it deserves." Tony McAleavy, director of research and development at the Education Development Trust, said: "The reduction in pupils opting for GCSE and A-level languages is concerning, particularly coupled with teachers' lack of faith in the exam system." "Solutions are required to give languages a firmer place in the curriculum, to make languages more compelling for pupils who find the examination process a barrier and to boost teacher morale."

Questions 1–8

Reading Passage 1 has eight paragraphs, **A–H.**

Choose the most suitable paragraph headings from the list of headings and write the correct letter, **A–H,** in boxes 1–8 on your answer sheet.

1. Data about studying [　　　]
2. Stable results [　　　]
3. Heavy economic losses [　　　]
4. Fairness of the exams [　　　]
5. A hard option [　　　]
6. A-level changes [　　　]
7. The most important thing for languages to be able to prosper [　　　]
8. Weak influence on pupils [　　　]

Questions 9–13

Classify the events with the following dates.

A. 2018

B. 2016

C. 2014–2015

D. None of the above

In boxes 9–13 on your answer sheet, write either **A, B, C** or **D.**

9. A Drop of GCSE to 48% [   ]

10. New syllabus system arrives in England [   ]

11. The start of new exams [   ]

12. The rise in entries [   ]

13. The decline of French by 1 percent [   ]

READING PASSAGE 2

Making Sense of Scent

With every whiff you take as you walk by a bakery, a cloud of chemicals comes swirling up your nose. Identifying the smell as freshly baked bread is a complicated process. But, compared to the other senses, the sense of smell is often underappreciated.

In a survey of 7,000 young people around the world, about half of those between the age of 16 and 30 said that they would rather lose their sense of smell than give up access to technology like laptops or cell phones.

We're not that acutely aware of our use of olfaction in daily living. In fact, mammals have about a thousand genes that code for odor reception. And even though humans have far fewer active odor receptor genes, 5 percent of our DNA is devoted to olfaction, a fact that emphasizes how important our sense of smell is.

Smell begins at the back of nose, where millions of sensory neurons lie in a strip of tissue called the olfactory epithelium. Molecules of odorants pass through the superior nasal concha of the nasal passages and come down on the epithelium. The tips of the epithelium cells contain proteins called receptors that bind odor molecules. The receptors are like locks and the keys to open these locks are the odor molecules that float past, explains Leslie Vosshall, a scientist who studies olfaction.

People have about 450 different types of olfactory receptors. (For comparison, dogs have about two times as many.) Each receptor can be activated by many different odor molecules, and each odor molecule can activate several different types of receptors. However, the forces that bind receptors and odor molecules can vary greatly in strength, so that some interactions are better "fits" than others.

The complexity of receptors and their interactions with odor molecules are what allow us to detect a wide variety of smells. And what we think of as a single smell is actually a combination of many odor molecules acting on a variety of receptors, creating an intricate neural code that we can identify as the scent of a rose or freshly-cut grass.

This neural code begins with the nose's sensory neurons. Once an odor molecule binds to a receptor, it initiates an electrical signal that travels from the sensory neurons to the olfactory bulb, a structure at the base of the forebrain that relays the signal to other brain areas for additional processing.

One of these areas is the piriform cortex, a collection of neurons located just behind the olfactory bulb that works to identify the smell. Smell information also goes to the thalamus, a structure that serves as a relay station for all of the sensory information coming into the brain. The thalamus transmits some of this smell information to the orbitofrontal cortex, where it can then be integrated with taste information. What we often attribute to the sense of taste is actually the result of this sensory integration.

"The olfactory system is critical when we're appreciating the foods and beverages we consume," says Monell Chemical Senses Centre scientist Charles Wysocki. This coupling of smell and taste explains why foods seem lacklustre with a head cold.

You've probably experienced that a scent can also conjure up emotions and even specific memories, like when a whiff of cologne at a department store reminds you of your favorite uncle who wears the same scent. This happens because the thalamus sends smell information to the hippocampus and amygdala, key brain regions involved in learning and memory.

Although scientists used to think that the human nose could identify about 10,000 different smells, Vosshall and her colleagues have recently shown that people can identify far more scents. Starting with 128 different odor molecules, they made random mixtures of 10, 20, and 30 odor molecules, so many that the smell produced was unrecognizable to participants. The researchers then presented people with three vials, two of which contained identical mixtures while the third contained a different concoction and asked them to pick out the smell that didn't belong.

Predictably, the more overlap there was between two types of mixtures, the harder they were to tell apart. After calculating how many of the mixtures the majority of people could tell apart, the researchers were able to predict how people would fare if presented with every possible mixture that could be created from the 128 different odour molecules.

They used this data to estimate that the average person can detect at least one trillion different smells, a far cry from the previous estimate of 10,000.

This number is probably an underestimation of the true number of smells we can detect, said Vosshall, because there are far more than 128 different types of odour molecules in the world. And our olfaction is quite powerful comparing to other mammals. For example, marine animals can detect only water-soluble odorants.

No longer should humans be considered poor smellers. "It's time to give our sense of smell the recognition it deserves," said Vosshall.

Questions 14–19

Do the following statements agree with the information given in Reading Passage 1?

In boxes 14–19 on your answer sheet, write

TRUE if the statement agrees with the information

FALSE if the statement contradicts the information

NOT GIVEN if there is no information on this

14. In general, olfaction and sense of taste are considered equally important. [   ]

15. About 7,000 young people around the world would prefer losing their sense of smell than access to laptops. [   ]

16. Odor reception is an integral function of all mammals. [   ]

17. Superior nasal concha is compared to a lock and odor molecules are like keys that are used to open it. [   ]

18. Cats have two times as many olfactory receptors as humans. [   ]

19. We are able to detect a lot of different scents because of a variety of odor receptors, which translate impact of molecules into a neural code. [   ]

Questions 20–25

Complete the sentences below.

Write **NO MORE THAN TWO WORDS** from the passage for each answer.

Write your answers in boxes 20–25 on your answer sheet.

20. The part of our brain responsible for identifying the smell is called ⬚.

21. The ⬚ is a region in our brain that serves as a transition station for all sensory information that we receive.

22. Sense of smell is closely related to ⬚.

23. ⬚ and ⬚ are involved in arousing memories caused by specific smells.

24. The experiment proved that the average person can discriminate between at least ⬚ smells.

25. Sea mammals can smell only odorants that are ⬚ in water.

READING PASSAGE 3

Cognitive Dissonance

A. Charles Darwin said, "This not the strongest of the species that survive, nor the most intelligent, but the one most responsive to change." So, you've sold your home, quit your job, shunned your colleagues, abandoned your friends and family. The end of the world is nigh, and you 'know for a fact' that you are one of the chosen few who will be swept up from the 'great flood' approaching on 21st December at midnight to be flown to safety on a far-off planet. And then midnight on 21st December comes around and there is no flood. No end of the world. No flying saucer to the rescue. What do you do? Admit you were wrong? Acknowledge that you gave up position, money, friends – for nothing? Tell yourself and others you have been a schmuck? Not on your life.

B. Social psychologist Leon Festinger infiltrated a flying saucer doomsday cult in the late 1950s. The members of this cult had given up everything on the premise that the world was about to self-destruct and that they, because of their faith, would be the sole survivors. In the lead up to the fateful day, the cult shunned publicity and shied away from journalists. Festinger posed as a cultist and was present when the space ship failed to show up. He was curious about what would happen. How would the disappointed cultists react to the failure of their prophecy? Would they be embarrassed and humiliated? What actually happened amazed him.

C. Now, after the non-event, the cultists suddenly wanted publicity. They wanted media attention and coverage. Why? So, they could explain how their faith and obedience had helped save the planet from the flood. The aliens had spared planet earth for their sake – and now their new role was to spread the word and make us all listen. This fascinated Festinger. He observed that the real driving force behind the cultists' apparently inexplicable response was the need, not to face the awkward and uncomfortable truth and 'change their minds,' but rather to 'make minds comfortable' – to smooth over the unacceptable inconsistencies.

D. Festinger coined the term 'cognitive dissonance' to describe the uncomfortable tension we feel when we experience conflicting thoughts or beliefs (cognitions) or engage in behaviour that is apparently opposed to our stated beliefs. What is particularly interesting is the lengths to which people will go to reduce the inner tension without accepting that they might, in fact, be wrong. They will accept almost any form of relief, other than admitting being at fault, or mistaken. Festinger quickly realized that our intolerance for 'cognitive dissonance' could explain many mysteries of human behavior.

E. In a fascinating experiment Festinger and his colleagues paid some subjects twenty dollars to tell a specific lie, while they paid another group of subjects only one dollar to do the same. Those who were paid just one dollar were far more likely to claim, after the event, that they had actually believed in the lie they were told to tell. Why? Well, because it's just so much harder to justify having done something that conflicts with your own sense of being 'an honest person' for a mere pittance. If you get more money, you can tell yourself: 'Yeah, I lied, but I got well paid! It was justified.' But for one dollar? That's not a good enough reason to lie, so what you were saying must have been true in the first place, right?

F. Emotional factors influence how we vote for our politicians much more than our careful and logical appraisal of their policies, according to Drew Westen, a professor of psychiatry and psychology. This may come as little surprise to you, but what about when we learn that our favored politician may be dishonest? Do we take the trouble to really find out what they are supposed to have done, and so possibly have to change our opinions (and our vote), or do we experience that nasty cognitive dissonance and so seek to keep our minds comfortable at the possible cost of truth?

G. Cognitive dissonance is essentially a matter of commitment to the choices one has made, and the ongoing need to satisfactorily justify that commitment, even in the face of convincing but conflicting evidence. This is why it can take a long time to leave a cult or an abusive relationship – or even to stop smoking. Life's commitments, whether to a job, a social cause, or a romantic partner, require heavy emotional investment, and so carry significant emotional risks. If people didn't keep to their commitments, they would experience uncomfortable emotional tension. In a way, it makes sense that our brains should be hard-wired for monitoring and justifying our choices and actions – so as to avoid too much truth breaking in at once and overwhelming us.

H. I guess we can't really develop unless we start to get a grip and have some personal honesty about what really motivates us. This is part of genuine maturity. If I know I am being lazy, and can admit it to myself, that at least is a first step to correcting it. If, however, I tell myself it's more sensible to wait before vacuuming, then I can go around with a comfortable self-concept of 'being sensible' while my filthy carpets and laziness remain unchanged. Cognitive dissonance can actually help me mature, if I can bring myself, first, to notice it (making it conscious) and second, to be more open to the message it brings me, in spite of the discomfort. As dissonance increases, providing I do not run away into self-justification, I can get a clearer and clearer sense of what has changed, and what I need to do about it. And then I can remember what Darwin had to say about who will survive...

Questions 26–33

Reading Passage 3 has eight paragraphs, **A–H**. Choose the most suitable headings for these paragraphs from the list of ten headings below. Write the appropriate number **i–x** in the text boxes **26–33**. There are more paragraph headings than paragraphs, so you will not use them all.

List of Headings

   i. Leon Festinger: On being stood up by the aliens

  ii. Dishonest politicians? Never!

 iii. Mind manipulation: the true reason of strange behaviour

  iv. You can't handle the truth!

   v. The catastrophe of 21st December

  vi. Grow up—make cognitive dissonance work for you

 vii. How many dollars would you take to tell a lie?

viii. Revealing mysteries: Darwin was right.

 ix. Cognitive dissonance: who are you kidding?

  x. The high cost of commitment exposes us to cognitive dissonance

26. Passage A [   ]

27. Passage B [   ]

28. Passage C [   ]

29. Passage D [   ]

30. Passage E [   ]

31. Passage F [   ]

32. Passage G [   ]

33. Passage H [   ]

Questions 34–40

Choose the correct letter, **A, B** or **C**

Write the correct letter in boxes **34–40** on your answer sheet.

34. After the space ship didn't show up on the fateful day, the members of the flying saucer doomsday cult

    A. ☐ didn't want to admit the uncomfortable truth and still believed that the world would self-destruct.

    B. ☐ were embarrassed and humiliated because of their failure.

    C. ☐ wanted media attention to say that they had saved the planet.

35. The main reason why people fight cognitive dissonance is

    A. ☐ a desire to reduce inner tension.

    B. ☐ people's unwillingness to accept their mistakes.

    C. ☐ wish to avoid the awkward feeling of lying without a good reason.

36. During the experiment, people who were telling lies were more likely to claim that they believed in the lie if

A. ☐ they were paid less.

B. ☐ they were paid more.

C. ☐ they felt uncomfortable lying.

37. Commitment to the choices someone has made, and the ongoing need to justify that commitment despite the conflicting evidence, can be explained by the fact that

A. ☐ it causes uncomfortable emotional tension.

B. ☐ commitments require heavy emotional investment.

C. ☐ our brain always justifies our choices.

38. The major part of genuine maturity is the ability of

A. ☐ sensible reasoning.

B. ☐ disregarding cognitive dissonance.

C. ☐ being honest with yourself.

39. According to the text, which of the situations below is NOT an example of cognitive dissonance?

A. ☐ A man learns that his favourite politician is dishonest but continues to vote for him.

B. ☐ A woman doesn't want to vacuum but convinces herself that otherwise her carpet will remain filthy and finally does it.

C. ☐ A woman has been dating her boyfriend for five years. Everyone tells her that it's an abusive relationship because he often beats and humiliates her but she doesn't want to leave her romantic partner.

40. Charles Darwin's quote from the beginning of the text implies that

A. ☐ cognitive dissonance helps us change and therefore makes us more enduring species.

B. ☐ people often accept almost any form of relief, rather than admitting being at fault, to survive.

C. ☐ fighting the discomfort caused by cognitive dissonance is a survival mechanism developed during the evolution.

Answers

1. D	21. Thalamus
2. F	22. Sense of taste
3. H	23. Hippocampus, Amygdala
4. G	24. One trillion
5. A	25. Soluble
6. B	26. v
7. E	27. i
8. C	28. ix
9. C	29. iv
10. B	30. vii
11. A	31. ii
12. D	32. x
13. C	33. vi
14. Not Given	34. C
15. False	35. A
16. True	36. A
17. False	37. B
18. Not Given	38. C
19. True	39. B
20. Piriform cortex	40. A

Hands-On

READING PASSAGE 1

The Animal that Regrows Its Head

In a windowless lab at the University of Galway in Ireland, there's a fish tank containing an extraordinary creature. Perched on blue cocktail sticks like lollipops, rows of seashells are coated in a strange "living hair," buffeted by gently flowing seawater. This colony of tiny marine animals – known as "snail fur" – was harvested in Irish rockpools off the backs of hermit crabs, and is related to jellyfish, corals and sea anemones.

Each no bigger than a baby's eyelash, they are called Hydractinia, and up close resemble a tree, each with a foot, a trunk and a tentacled head used for catching tasty passing detritus. They also have a superpower: when grazing fish frequently bite off those tentacle heads, they re-sprout to their former hirsute glory within a week.

It's this talent that has captured the attention of Uri Frank and colleagues at Galway's Regenerative Medicine Institute. Along with a growing number of researchers, he claims that the tissue regeneration seen in creatures like Hydractinia could be an ancient power possessed by most animals, including humans – it's just dormant. So, how does this "snail fur" regrow itself? And could it hold the key to tissue regeneration in human beings too?

Many animals can regenerate body parts, from starfish to salamanders. But primitive snail fur is unusual, not least because its abilities are so extreme.

Marshalling Stem Cells

The key to Hydractinia's regenerative talent is the fact that it retains its embryonic stem cells for life. This means that any wound healing process doesn't just produce a scab and a scar but a whole new body part as it would in an embryo, even a head.

At a gathering of developmental biologists earlier this year, Frank showed a video of the creature's head-budding process in action, embryonic stem cells that had been genetically altered to glow green rushing to the neck end of a headless Hydractinia. Attendees were agog. As one tweeted: "Uri Frank shows time lapse movie of Hydractinia stem cells physically moving across to head (wound site) – Wow!"

Since recording that video the Galway team have been working to understand how Hydractinia rebuilds its severed body and hope to publish their findings shortly in a scientific journal. While they're keeping schtum about the details, the paper will focus on how the creature marshals its stem cells to regrow its head – for example, how stem cells know the head's missing – and where exactly the embryonic stem cells come from.

Studying Hydractinia has also led Frank and colleagues to ask a bigger question: why can only a few animals regenerate while most can't? A salamander can regrow a lost tail but closely related frogs can't regrow a lost limb. And if a tiny marine creature can regrow its own head, why can't humans even regrow their adult teeth? After all, says Frank, it's not as if human and Hydractinia stem cell systems are so very different.

Ancient Ancestor

Key stem cell processes are ancient and common to many animal species. For instance, the complex "Wnt" signalling system, which controls stem cells in developing embryos and, when uncontrolled, causes cancer, is very similar in all animals, including Hydractinia and people. It's one of a handful of complex stem cell systems, each involving hundreds of elements, which have remained the same since Hydractinia branched off the evolutionary tree that eventually led to us around 600 million years ago.

Over the past decade or so, researchers have started to believe that stem cells first evolved in a creature even more ancient than Hydractinia, whose soft body has long since dissolved in ancient seabeds. In this as-yet-unknown creature, the power of regeneration may have first evolved, says Frank, endowing all later animals with a basic toolkit for regrowing lost body parts – one which mainly lies dormant in present-day life.

"It's maybe not such a crazy idea. Stem cell systems are enormously complex and 600 million years may not be long enough to reinvent another system from scratch. So, it's more likely to believe that our stem cell system and Hydractinia's stem cell system were actually inherited from a common ancestor," says Frank. "And if you think about it, Hydractinia can grow a new head and, although we cannot as adults, we can do that as embryos when we make our own head. So, it is possible that this ability to do so is switched off in human adults and in Hydractinia it's not."

This theory ties in with a study published last year in the journal Nature, about two varieties of an ancient form of flatworm, the planarian. This worm has been studied for over a century because of its amazing regenerative powers. Slice them up into tiny pieces and some planarian worms can regrow their bodies from even the tiniest tailpiece. Others need most of their body intact to regrow a head. Until now, that is.

Researchers at the Max Planck Institute tested the idea that all planarian flatworms have the same regenerative superpowers but that in some it's switched off early in development. They were right. With a relatively simple tweak to the stem cell system of a developing embryo they turned a creature that in nature couldn't regrow a head out of a tiny tailpiece, into one that could.

In Galway, Frank hopes his research will help to explain the apparently miraculous results from planarian experiments and unravel other mysteries, too. Why, for instance, do planarians easily grow new tails when Hydractinia struggles to regrow its foot? One idea is that body symmetry – front/back or left-right as in planarians and humans but not snail fur – may dictate where stem cells in the body can migrate to.

In theory, it's possible that humans may harbour the same dormant regenerative superpowers as snail fur and flatworms, however far they seem from humans. At the most basic cellular level there are striking similarities. Studying them could teach us how to regrow damaged or lost body parts too. "While there's no market for regrowing human heads," says Frank, "wouldn't it be great if we could repair spinal cords, damaged hearts, damaged kidneys, hands and any other organs we might lose?"

The flatworm studies imply this might not be quite as unthinkable as once thought. The Victorian father of regenerative science, Thomas Hunt Morgan carried out flatworm experiments showed their amazing powers to regrow a whole body from a stump in 1901. But he abandoned the study, writing: "We will never understand the phenomena of development and regeneration."

Clearly, there are many mysteries of regeneration still to be revealed, yet now it seems that a tiny creature living in a fish tank in Galway and its ilk could help us unlock the bizarre process of regrowing body parts sooner than we thought.

Questions 1–5

Do the following statements agree with the information in the IELTS reading text?

In boxes **1–5** on your answer sheet, write

TRUE if the statement agrees with the information

FALSE if the statement contradicts the information

NOT GIVEN if there is no information on this

1. "Snail fur" is related to jellyfish, corals and sea anemones.

2. Judging by the picture, Hydractinia can regrow its head in a day.

3. Uri Frank thinks that even humans can possess regenerating powers.

4. Snail fur is similar to salamanders and starfish.

5. Healing in Hydractinia produces new body part.

Questions 6–9

Choose the correct letter, **A, B, C** or **D.**

Write the correct letter in boxes **6–9** on your answer sheet.

6. Which of the following **DIDN'T** happen at a gathering of developmental biologists?

   A. ☐ Uri Frank showed a video of Hydractinia regenerating its head.

   B. ☐ Some stem cells of the creature were glowing green.

   C. ☐ Attendants were astonished by the show.

   D. ☐ A research conference took place afterwards.

7. The Galway team will focus on what in their future paper?

   A. ☐ How Hydractinia manages to regrow its head.

   B. ☐ How stem cells know that the head is missing.

   C. ☐ Where the stem cells come from.

   D. ☐ All of the above.

8. According to Frank Uri and his team:

   A. ☐ human and Hydractinia stem cells are similar.

   B. ☐ most organisms can regenerate themselves.

   C. ☐ frogs can regrow lost limbs.

   D. ☐ salamanders and frogs are not closely related.

Questions 9–13

Complete the sentences below.

Write **ONLY ONE WORD** from the passage for each answer.

Write your answers in boxes **9–13** on your answer sheet.

9. "Wnt" signalling system can cause ☐ if uncontrolled.

10. Human and Hydractinia stem cells might actually be from a common ☐.

11. The thing that dictates where stem cells in the body can migrate to might be body ☐.

12. Humans might possibly harbour the same ☐ regenerative superpowers as snail fur and flatworms.

13. Thomas Hunt Morgan said that we will never understand the of ☐ development and regeneration.

READING PASSAGE 2

All the Ways Women Are Still Pressured to Put Family Before Career

A. There's no denying that women around the world have made great strides toward equality in the past century. One hundred years ago, women in the United States still didn't have the right to vote, and very few were allowed to pursue higher education or a meaningful career outside of their household duties. Fast forward to today, and more than 70 percent of women between the ages of 20 and 54 are active members of the national workforce. On top of this, 2015 marked the first year when women were, on average, more likely to have a bachelor's degree than men, and this trend is on the rise.

B. But despite all this newfound opportunity, the prevailing societal attitudes about what women are historically supposed to value still have a long way to go. That's why we've partnered with SK-II to learn more about all of the ways women are still pressured to stick to outdated gender norms. "Women have won unprecedented rights thanks to the feminist movement, but as a society, we still expect women to prioritize family over career, or even over their own needs," says Silvia Dutchevici, president and founder of the Critical Therapy Center in New York City. Dutchevici says many women feel pressure to "have it all," meaning both a thriving career and the perfect family, but that can be very difficult to achieve.

C. "Most women try to balance work and family," Dutchevici says, "but that balance is seldom equal." In fact, she says working mothers — even those with partners — often find themselves essentially working two full-time jobs: keeping their career together while doing the brunt of housework, cooking and child-rearing. This happens for a variety of reasons, but societal expectations about the roles of women and men at home are still very much to blame, says Tamra Lashchyk, a Wall Street executive, business coach and author of the book "Lose the Gum: A Survival Guide to Women on Wall Street."

D. "No matter how successful she is, the burden of running a household still falls on the woman's shoulders," Lashchyk says. "Men get more of a pass when it comes to these duties, especially those that involve children." Lashchyk says much of this pressure on women to conform to a more domestic lifestyle comes from friends and family.

E. "In many people's minds, a woman's career success pales in comparison to having a family," she says. "Especially if the woman is single, no matter how great her professional achievements, almost every single one of her conversations with her family will include questions about her romantic life or lack thereof. I could literally tell my family I'd cured cancer and the conversation would still end with, 'But are you dating anyone?'" While covert societal expectations might contribute to some of this inequality, workplace policies on maternity and paternity leave can hold a lot of the blame.

F. "Unfortunately, many workplace policies regarding taking time off to care for family do not the changing times," Dutchevici says. "Both men and women suffer in their careers when they prioritize family, but women carry far harsher punishments. Their choice to take time off and start a family can result in lower pay, and fewer promotions in the future. The right to family leave is not a woman's issue, it is a society's issue, a family's issue." Lashchyk agrees with this sentiment. "There should be more flexibility and benefits [in the workplace], like longer periods of time for paternity leave… If paternity leave was extended, men could share a greater responsibility in child care, and they could also spend more time bonding with their infant children, which is beneficial for the entire family.

G. Another less visible way the modern workplace forces women to choose family over career has to do with the fact that women are pushing back pregnancy, says Jeni Mayorskaya, a fertility expert and CEO of Stork Club, an online community for women dedicated to fertility issues. "Compared to our parents, our generation is having children a decade later," Mayorskaya says. "Unfortunately, when we hit our mid-30s and we're finally ready for that managing position or that title of a partner at a firm we fought so hard for, we have to think about putting our career on pause and becoming a mom."

H. So, what can women do to combat these societal pressures? Finding workplaces that offer flexible schedules, work-at-home opportunities and ample maternity and paternity leave is a good first step, but Dr. Neeta Bhushan, an emotional intelligence advocate and author, says women should also learn to put themselves first. "The first step is being mindful of your emotional health in your relationships with others and the relationship you have with yourself, "Bhushan says. "When you put yourself first, you are able to make a bigger impact on your community. This is different than being selfish—think beyond you. You want to make sure that you are being taken care of so that you can take care of others."

Questions 14–21

Reading Passage 2 has eight paragraphs, **A–H.**

Which paragraph contains the following information?

Write the correct letter, **A–H,** in boxes 14–21 on your answer sheet.

14. Two "jobs" that women essentially do [   ]

15. Question about dating [   ]

16. Delaying pregnancy [   ]

17. The first year, when women are more likely to have bachelor's a degree [   ]

18. The reasons to put yourself first [   ]

19. The source of conformation to domestic lifestyle [   ]

20. Our expectancy over women's prioritization [   ]

21. Pros of extended paternity [   ]

Questions 22–27

Choose the correct letter, **A, B, C** or **D.**

Write the correct letter in boxes 22–27 on your answer sheet.

22. One hundred years ago, women in USA:

   A. [ ] had no rights.

   B. [ ] were not allowed to pursue higher education.

   C. [ ] couldn't vote.

   D. [ ] were members of the national workforce.

23. According to Silvia Dutchevici:

A. ☐ feminist movement has more disadvantages than advantages.

B. ☐ we now expect women to prioritize their career over family.

C. ☐ we now expect women to prioritize their own needs over family.

D. ☐ women rarely achieve equal balance between family and work.

24. Tamra Lashchyk, a Wall Street executive, says that

A. ☐ most women are still responsible for household duties.

B. ☐ men don't really need to do any housework.

C. ☐ it's more important for a woman to have a career than a family.

D. ☐ both A and B.

25. Lashchyk agrees with Dutchevici on

A. ☐ women's rights and feminism.

B. ☐ the fact that the right to family leave is a societal issue.

C. ☐ the state of women's rights in America.

D. ☐ the reason why women want to pursue their careers.

26. Jeni Mayorskaya says that

A. ☐ nowadays women give birth later than they used to.

B. ☐ now women don't push back against pregnancy.

C. ☐ when women are in their 30s, they have to think about putting their career on pause to become a mother.

D. ☐ Both A and C.

27. According to the last paragraph, how can women deal with societal pressure?

A. ☐ They should be selfish.

B. ☐ They shouldn't work at home.

C. ☐ They should put themselves first.

D. ☐ They should avoid marriage entirely.

READING PASSAGE 3

The Real Risks of Artificial Intelligence

If you believe some AI-watchers, we are racing towards the Singularity – a point at which artificial intelligence outstrips our own and machines go on to improve themselves at an exponential rate. If that happens – and it's a big if – what will become of us?

In the last few years, several high-profile voices, from Stephen Hawking to Elon Musk and Bill Gates have warned that we should be more concerned about possible dangerous outcomes of supersmart AI. And they've put their money where their mouth is: Musk is among several billionaire backers of OpenAI, an organisation dedicated to developing AI that will benefit humanity.

But for many, such fears are overblown. As Andrew Ng at Stanford University, who is also chief scientist at Chinese internet giant Baidu, puts it: fearing a rise of killer robots is like worrying about overpopulation on Mars.

That's not to say our increasing reliance on AI does not carry real risks, however. In fact, those risks are already here. As smart systems become involved in ever more decisions in arenas ranging from healthcare to finance to criminal justice, there is a danger that important parts of our lives are being made without sufficient scrutiny. What's more, AIs could have knock-on effects that we have not prepared for, such as changing our relationship with doctors to the way our neighbourhoods are policed.

What exactly is AI? Very simply, it's machines doing things that are considered to require intelligence when humans do them: understanding natural language, recognising faces in photos, driving a car, or guessing what other books we might like based on what we have previously enjoyed reading. It's the difference between a mechanical arm on a factory production line programmed to repeat the same basic task over and over again, and an arm that learns through trial and error how to handle different tasks by itself.

How is AI helping us? The leading approach to AI right now is machine learning, in which programs are trained to pick out and respond to patterns in large amounts of data, such as identifying a face in an image or choosing a winning move in the board game Go. This technique can be applied to all sorts of problems, such as getting computers to spot patterns in medical images, for example. Google's artificial intelligence company DeepMind are collaborating with the UK's National Health Service in a handful of projects, including ones in which their software is being taught to diagnose cancer and eye disease from patient scans. Others are using machine learning to catch early signs of conditions such as heart disease and Alzheimer.

Artificial intelligence is also being used to analyse vast amounts of molecular information looking for potential new drug candidates – a process that would take humans too long to be worth doing. Indeed, machine learning could soon be indispensable to healthcare.

Artificial intelligence can also help us manage highly complex systems such as global shipping networks. For example, the system at the heart of the Port Botany container terminal in Sydney manages the movement of thousands of shipping containers in and out of the port, controlling a fleet of automated, driverless straddle-carriers in a completely human-free zone. Similarly, in the mining industry, optimisation engines are increasingly being used to plan and coordinate the movement of a resource, such as iron ore, from initial transport on huge driverless mine trucks, to the freight trains that take the ore to port.

AIs are at work wherever you look, in industries from finance to transportation, monitoring the share market for suspicious trading activity or assisting with ground and air traffic control. They even help to keep spam out of your inbox. And this is just the beginning for artificial intelligence. As the technology advances, so too does the number of applications.

So, what's the problem? Rather than worrying about a future AI takeover, the real risk is that we can put too much trust in the smart systems we are building. Recall that machine learning works by training software to spot patterns in data. Once trained, it is then put to work analysing fresh, unseen data. But when the computer spits out an answer, we are typically unable to see how it got there.

There are obvious problems here. A system is only as good as the data it learns from. Take a system trained to learn which patients with pneumonia had a higher risk of death, so that they might be admitted to hospital. It inadvertently classified patients with asthma as being at lower risk. This was because in normal situations, people with pneumonia and a history of asthma go straight to intensive care and therefore get the kind of treatment that significantly reduces their risk of dying. The machine learning took this to mean that asthma + pneumonia = lower risk of death.

As AIs are rolled out to assess everything from your credit rating to suitability for a job you are applying for to criminals' chance of reoffending, the risks that they will sometimes get it wrong – without us necessarily knowing – get worse.

Since so much of the data that we feed AIs is imperfect, we should not expect perfect answers all the time. Recognising that is the first step in managing the risk. Decision-making processes built on top of AIs need to be made more open to scrutiny. Since we are building artificial intelligence in our own image, it is likely to be both as brilliant and as flawed as we are.

Questions 28–36

Complete the sentences below.

Write **NO MORE THAN TWO WORDS** from the passage for each answer.

Write your answers in boxes 28–36 on your answer sheet.

28. The singularity is the point where AI [   ] our own machines.

29. Many people, including Stephen Hawking, Elon Musk and Bill Gates, warned us about possible [   ] of super-smart AI.

30. According to Andrew Ng, fearing a rise of [   ] is similar to worrying about overpopulation on Mars.

31. There is a danger that many important parts of our lives, like healthcare, finance and [   ] will be without sufficient scrutiny.

32. Simply put, AI is machines doing things that are considered to require [   ] when humans do them.

33. Nowadays, the main approach to AI is [   ].

34. DeepMind, in collaboration with the UK's National Health Service, works on many projects, including the one where software learns how to [   ] and eye disease.

35. In the nearest future machine learning could be [＿＿＿＿＿＿＿] to healthcare.

36. AI might also help in managing [＿＿＿＿＿＿] networks.

Questions 37–40

Do the following statements agree with the information given in Reading Passage 3?

In boxes 37–40 on your answer sheet, write

TRUE if the statement agrees with the information

FALSE if the statement contradicts the information

NOT GIVEN if there is no information on this

37. AI works in many different industries nowadays. [＿＿＿＿＿]

38. We shouldn't put too much trust in AI in the future. [＿＿＿＿＿]

39. The quality of the data doesn't affect the ability of AI to learn information correctly. [＿＿＿＿＿]

40. We can get perfect answers from AI all the time. [＿＿＿＿＿]

Answers

1. True	**11.** Symmetry
2. False	**12.** Dormant
3. True	**13.** Phenomena
4. Not Given	**14.** C
5. True	**15.** E
6. D	**16.** G
7. D	**17.** A
8. A	**18.** H
9. Cancer	**19.** D
10. Ancestor	**20.** B

21. F

22. C

23. D

24. A

25. B

26. D

27. C

28. Outstrips

29. Dangerous outcomes

30. Killer robots

31. Criminal justice

32. Intelligence

33. Machine learning

34. Diagnose cancer

35. Indispensable

36. Global shipping

37. True/li>

38. Not Given

39. False

40. False

GENERAL
TRAINING

General Training
Reading 2

Read the Text and Answer Questions 1–8.

Your Guide to Renting Accommodation in Stonington

This leaflet has been developed by the Stonington City Council to assist migrants and students who have arrived in Stonington and are looking to rent long-term accommodation. The City of Stonington has 5 suburbs and in terms of accommodation, the suburbs vary significantly.

A. Richmond

Richmond is the busiest and most expensive suburb in Stonington. Richmond Business Park hosts a total of 56 industries that employ approximately 5500 people which creates a steady demand for accommodation in this area. From 2 to 20 stories, 1, 2 and 3 bedroom apartment-style living is the most common type of accommodation in Richmond. Depending upon the number of bedrooms, rental prices range from $1600 to $2500 per month.[7] **Richmond is well-known for its cosmopolitan environment.**

B. Crane Hills

This suburb is located in the southern hills of Stonington.[4] **The suburb offers a brilliant outlook over the city.** Accommodation is mostly duplex houses and bungalows. Rent ranges from $2,000 to $3,000 a month. The largest park in Stonington is located here, along with a golf course, jogging track and children's playground. The government has undertaken to expand the residential area through the western section of the hill and this development will be completed by next year.[1] **It is anticipated that the building of around 500 new houses will commence (start) early in the new year.**

C. Blackburn

Although Blackburn is the smallest suburb in Stonington it has the most dwellings. A suburb of mostly independent houses, rental prices for 1, 2 and 3 bedroom houses range from $1500 to $2000 per month. Most homes are spacious with large backyards[8] **however, rental accommodation in the area is not readily available** and[2] **what becomes available is quickly snapped up!** Most tenants of rental homes commit to a minimum 3-year lease. There is one primary school, a train station and a shopping centre in the area.

D. Malvern

Famous for its racecourse, Stonington's oldest suburb is Malvern. Most of the houses in this suburb are renovated—rent for a 2 and 3 bedroom home runs at around $800 and $1200 respectively.[6] **Homes built in Malvern typically do not have any yards (outdoor living area).** Facilities include one supermarket, two shopping centres and the Stonington Community Hospital. At the moment, there is no school although the state government is reviewing a proposal to build one.

E. Caulfield

Closest to the city centre and with most government department offices, is Caulfield.[5] **A variety of mixed accommodation options from apartments to houses are available in Caulfield.** Caulfield does not have a train station, but its bus system is comprehensive.[3] **Caulfield is very**

much in a growth phase, so a large portion of available accommodation is newly-completed and modern. A spacious 3 bedroom house will cost around $1500 a month, while a 3 bedroom apartment averages around $1200 per month. Caulfield has 2 schools and 3 supermarkets, and accommodation in the suburb is typically good value for money.

Questions 1–8

Look at the descriptions (A-E) of the five suburbs in Stonington.

For which suburb are the following statements true?

Write the correct letter, A-E, in boxes 1–8 on your answer sheet.

NB: You may use any letter more than once.

1. This suburb is expecting new buildings in the near future. **(B)**

2. This suburb is the most popular rental area in Stonington. **(C)**

3. This suburb has mostly new places to live in. **(E)**

4. This suburb offers great views. **(B)**

5. This suburb offers a variety of different housing options. **(E)**

6. The accommodation in this suburb has limited outdoor living areas. **(D)**

7. This suburb is influenced by many different countries. **(A)**

8. This suburb has the lowest level of housing availability. **(C)**

Read the Text and Answer Questions 9–14.

Blossom Child Care

Service Information and Fees

Blossom Child Care (BCC) is a privately owned child care centre which has been operating in five locations in Wales for the past 10 years. Our services cater for children aged from 1 to 6 years old. We have a range of child care service to suit the needs of working parents. As an associate member of the National Child Care Institute, all our employees are highly qualified.

We offer three levels of childcare:

I. Pre-Kindergarten

Children under two are in the Pre-Kindergarten group. BCC's Teddy, Kinda and Koala rooms have been allocated for this age group where we accommodate 15 children per room. We provide special care and make sure that one of our highly qualified senior supervisors, in addition to three general staff, are always available in each room. Please ensure your child has at least 4 nappies and 2 additional sets of clothes every day.

Food: In addition to cow's milk, if your child is on solid food, we provide a nutritional blend of fruits and vegetables. If your child is on formula, please inform us.

Toys: All Pre-Kindergarten rooms have toilet training toys which, along with other general toys, are always maintained at the strictest hygiene standards.

Fees: Our Pre-Kindergarten service fee is $300 per week with a one-off registration fee of $30. Fees are payable weekly.

II. Kindergarten

Children aged two to four are in the Kindergarten group. BCC has four allocated rooms for this group each accommodates 20 children. Two staff are on duty in each room and one senior supervisor is in charge of all four rooms.

Food: Children are provided with three full meals a day. [9] **All meals are cooked on the premises by a child food specialist and the menus are rotated so that your child gets the right nutritional balance.** [14] **If your child is allergic to any food, please inform us by filling in the Food Allergy Form (IN WRITING).**

Toys: Our Kindergarten rooms are decorated with educational posters and are full of learning games and puzzles. We discourage children bringing their own toys from home as they are often a source of contention and argument.

Fees: The Kindergarten service fee is $250 per week with a one-off registration fee of $40. Fees are payable weekly.

III. Post-Kindergarten

Children aged four to six are in the Post-Kindergarten group. We have two dedicated rooms for this group all decorated with artwork designed to stimulate learning. Each room accommodates 20 children and is serviced solely by one general staff member. [11] **BCC arranges one excursion (OUTING) session for this group every four weeks (1 MONTH).** [12] **The venues are generally parks, playgrounds, picnic-spots and the local zoo.** As a legal requirement, parents must fill in an Excursion Declaration Form before each trip which authorizes the Centre to take their children from the premises.

Food: Children in the Post-Kindergarten program get three meals a day – mostly meals with rice, vegetables and chicken. Please speak to your child's supervisor if you have any special dietary requirements.

Toys: There are four life-sized cartoon toys in each room along with a large variety of books.

Fees: The Post-Kindergarten service fee is $200 per week with a one-off registration fee of $40. Fees are payable weekly.

Questions 9–14

Classify each of the descriptions 9–14 as belonging to either A, B, C or D below.

Write your answers in boxes 9–14 on your answer sheet.

Groups	
A	Pre-Kindergarten
B	Kindergarten
C	Post-Kindergarten
D	Does not belong to any group

9. A variety of prepared food is offered. **(B)**

10. If needed, additional clothing is provided. **(D)**

11. An outing is arranged once a month. **(C)**

12. Children can see live animals. **(C)**

13. A student report is included. **(D)**

14. Any problems with diet should be dealt with in writing. **(B)**

SECTION 2

Questions 15–27

Read the Passage Below and Answer Questions 15–20.

THE ABC'S OF CV WRITING

Your Curriculum Vitae (CV) is one of the most important documents you will ever write. This summary of your academic and work history is an essential tool in your job search and commonly the first form of [15] **contact** with a potential employer.

With so many people in the job market it is your responsibility to 'sell' yourself, so before you put pen to paper, it is worthwhile taking time to carefully think about your [16] **approach.** To assist you in this process, we have listed the most common advice for preparing your CV below:

A. Your main goal is to demonstrate a match between your **accomplishments**[17] and the position you are applying for. The **job description**[18] will outline the qualifications and requisites for the position, so read it carefully.

B. Update your CV each time you apply for a job, specifically tailoring it to each position.

C. If you are applying for a position in another country, present your academic and work achievements in terms your future employer will understand and demonstrate your familiarity with the culture and business practices, where possible.

D. The format of your CV is always important. A clear, concise presentation will make your application stand out and be easier to read. A summary outlining your key strengths on page one will draw attention to your best features. The use of bullet points in the formatting can not only contribute to brevity but will also increase the impact of your CV.

E. Never send out a CV without a **cover letter**[19] highlighting the areas of your CV that particularly relate to the job being advertised.

F. In their enthusiasm for a particular position, some people may be tempted to exaggerate on their CVs. Employers are aware of this tendency and will check any claims you make concerning your experience, qualifications or remuneration levels. It pays to be truthful. If you are caught lying, your application will not be considered.

G. Grammatical and spelling errors are unacceptable in a CV, but they are one of the most common problems. Your CV must have no mistakes and must be attractively presented. A good strategy is to ask someone to check it for you before it is submitted to make sure it is error-free.

H. If you have difficulty writing your CV and feel that it will detract from your job application, there are **professional services**[20] that will assist you for a reasonable fee.

Questions 15–20

Complete each of the sentences below.

Choose **NO MORE THAN TWO WORDS** from the text for each answer.

Write your answers in boxes 15–20 on your answer sheet.

15. A CV is usually the initial **CONTACT** made with a future boss.

16. Writing a CV requires a well-considered **APPROACH.**

17. All **ACCOMPLISHMENTS** must show a relationship with the desired position.

18. The requirements of a position are explained in the **JOB DESCRIPTION.**

19. In addition to a CV, applications must also include a **COVER LETTER.**

20. If CV writing is too challenging, consider help from a **PROFESSIONAL SERVICE.**

Read the Text Below and Answer Questions 21–27.

WAITING AT JAKARTA MAHAL

When you finally hear the words 'Congratulations, you've been hired!' from the supervisor of the famous Jakarta Mahal Indian Restaurant, you might wonder, 'Now what do I do?'

On your first day you will be assigned to an experienced employee who will act as your adviser for the first week. Your mentor will also take you on a tour of the restaurant to familiarise you with the layout. Once you know where everything is and have met the staff, you will be advised of the daily routine. An important key to success is to memorise this and faithfully adhere to it.

Upon arrival at the restaurant, change into your [21]**uniform**—ensure it is ironed and stain-free. Depending on the time of the day, you may be required to lay the tables and stock the service areas with supplies of coffee, tea, clean tableware and linen. Once those tasks are complete, familiarise yourself with [22]**the menu** and any alterations made since you were last on duty. Pay particular attention to the daily specials and check the drinks menu and wine list. It may be necessary to consult with the [23]**head waiter** about the dishes on offer so you can answer queries, which could include describing cooking methods and ingredients.

Be on hand to greet the patrons, answer their questions, and escort them to their table. When everyone is [24]**seated** and has a menu, take their drink orders and inform them of the specials of the day. Be prepared to make recommendations if requested to do so.

Take the meal orders when the guests indicate they are ready and check to see if [25]**additional beverages** are needed. When the meals are ready they should be served quickly and efficiently.

A hallmark of an excellent waiter is table maintenance. During the meal ensure that empty glasses, dirty dishes and unused cutlery are removed. Also, be alert for anyone looking around in need of assistance.

Be sure to check [26]**the bill** before presenting it to the guests, making sure it is itemized and that the total and sales tax is correct. After you have collected payment and taken leave of your patrons, it is time to reset the table and [27]**begin again.**

Questions 21–27

Complete the flowchart below.

Choose **NO MORE THAN TWO WORDS** from the text for each answer.

Write your answers in boxes 21–27 on your answer sheet.

DAILY ACTIVITES AT JAKARTA MAHAL

Waiters must put on a clean 21 <u>**UNIFORM**</u>

↓

Become aware of any changes in 22 <u>**THE MENU**</u>

↓

Prepare for questions about the menu by talking to the 23 <u>**HEAD WAITER**</u>

↓

Tell guests about special after they have been 24 <u>**SEATED**</u>

↓

Once the meal order has been taken, inquire about 25 <u>**ADDITIONAL BEVERAGES**</u>

↓

Write all sales taxes on 26 <u>**THE BILL**</u>

↓

After the guests have left, 27 <u>**BEGIN AGAIN**</u>

SECTION 3

Read the Passage and Answer Questions 28–40.

New Impressions Bring Controversy

A. Many of history's pages reveal that renowned artists have often had to endure obstacles and criticisms before eventually rising to the heights of success in their careers. Nineteenth century artist Sir John Everett Millais is certainly one of them.

B. Born in 1829 in Southampton, England the youngest son of John William and Emily Mary Millais' two sons, John Everett showed extraordinary artistic talent from an early age. In time, the family moved to London and as residents, Everett's parents were determined to give young John an opportunity to develop his talent. A meeting with the president of the London Royal Academy of Art, Sir Martin Archer Shee, was arranged. It was not long before Sir Martin also saw the extraordinary natural artistic ability Everett possessed. As a result, in the summer of 1840 and at the age of 11, Everett became the youngest ever pupil to study art at the academy. [37]**His ability and age led to all his teachers affectionately referred to him as The Child. The extra attention shown to Everett eventually caused jealousy among his fellow students.** [32]**At the beginning of his studies Everett, a thinly-built boy,** [33]**often found it difficult to cope with the bullying he encountered at the art academy. However, as time went by and his peers became increasingly aware of his artistic talent – even in the complex area of portrait painting – bullying gave way to awe.**

C. Over the months and years Everett spent at the academy he began to concentrate on the theoretical aspects of art. [38]**His studies included reading the biographies of past great artists and almost all the books on art that the academy library had.** [29]**Interestingly, the reading and studying of most of these books was not needed in order to pass his exams. Everett, out of his genuine curiosity and passion for art, spent most of his leisure time at the library.** At the school's practical painting classes, he was well-known for going to considerable lengths to find the right elements needed for his painting – travelling long distances in search of the right natural scenes and paying large sums of money to hire models for his portrait painting. Over the course of his studies at the London Royal Academy of Art, he met two other like-minded artists – Holman Hunt and Gabriel Rossetti – who would later become his lifelong friends and key supporters of his artistic impressions.

D. In 1850, he held his first solo painting exhibition in London. It was a non-traditional exhibition in terms of style and pattern and proved to be controversial in terms of the subject matter displayed – the social class system. [39]**Everett displayed art on the topic of hierarchical or class distinctions between individuals and groups in English society.** [31]**Although a small portion of art lovers praised his exhibition,** he was strongly attacked by most of the art critics of the day. Some of his paintings on religious matters, which portrayed religion as something quite ordinary, made the conservative segment of the society angry.

E. [34]**Over the years, with the support of his two best friends Holman Hunt and Gabriel Rossetti, Everett started a movement which he named the Pre-Raphaelite Brotherhood (PRB).** [40]**The intention of his PRB movement was to reform art by rejecting the concept of the Renaissance1 movement which, he believed,** [35]**was a mechanical approach to art influenced by narrow academic teaching. Once the PRB movement was formally launched, attacks from art critics throughout England intensified. The PRB movement contradicted the views of almost all the other established artists in the country and led to John Ruskin,** the foremost art critic of that time, formally meeting Everett with the intention of persuading him to cease the PRB. Everett did not agree to give up his ideologies so no agreement between the two was reached. However, the incident had a direct consequence on Everett's personal life. Effie, Ruskin's wife, met Everett and over a period of time started to develop an attraction to him. Eventually Effie divorced Ruskin and married Everett.

F. Art historians today [28]**believe that the marriage of Everett and Effie acted as a catalyst in turning public opinion in his favour and inspired him to devote greater effort to his PRB movement.** In 1865, Everett finished a series of paintings based on his ideologies and in 1876 with such masterpieces as 'Twins', 'The Marquis of Salisbury' and 'The Lady Campbell' became the most successful portrait painter of the day.

G. In 1890, he was awarded the title of Sir and was made the president of the England Royal Art Academy. By that time, his works not only won the adoration of the masses in England but many other European countries as well. [30]**Unfortunately, shortly after being given the title of Sir, he fell ill and was wrongly diagnosed as having influenza. In 1894 it was discovered that he was actually suffering from cancer.** During July 1896, his situation became very critical and the queen of England personally contacted his doctors offering her full support. Sir John Everett however, passed away on the 13th of August in 1896.

H. A cultural movement from the 14th to the 17th century, which originated in Italy and spread all over Europe.

Questions 28–35

The passage has seven paragraphs A–G.

Which paragraph contains the following information?

Write the correct letter A–G in boxes 28–35 on your answer sheet.

N. B. You may use any letter more than once.

28. An event that led to a change in viewpoint. **(F)**

29. A positive example of doing more than what was required. **(C)**

30. An example of incorrect information being given. **(G)**

31. A minority that showed appreciation. **(D)**

32. An example of a positive change in human interaction. **(B)**

33. A description of Everett's physical appearance. **(B)**

34. An example of an official organizational beginning. **(E)**

35. An activity that was supposed to bring change. **(E)**

Questions 36–40

Do the following statements agree with the information given in the text?

In boxes 36–40 on your answer sheet, write

TRUE if the statement agrees with the information

FALSE if the statement contradicts the information

NOT GIVEN if there is no information on this

36. Everett's parents moved to London so he could study at the London Royal Academy. (**NOT GIVEN**)

37. In time, both his peers and teachers admired Everett. (**TRUE**)

38. As a youngster, Everett was interested in other artists. (**TRUE**)

39. Everett's first exhibition featured art about economic and social position. (**TRUE**)

40. Everett's plan for the PRB was to make art better. (**TRUE**)

Answers

1. B	**21.** uniform
2. C	**22.** the menu
3. E	**23.** head waiter
4. B	**24.** seated
5. E	**25.** additional beverages
6. D	**26.** the bill
7. A	**27.** begin again
8. C	**28.** F
9. B	**29.** C
10. D	**30.** G
11. C	**31.** D
12. C	**32.** B
13. D	**33.** B
14. B	**34.** E
15. contact	**35.** E
16. approach	**36.** NG
17. accomplishments	**37.** True
18. job description	**38.** True
19. covering letter	**39.** True
20. professional service	**40.** True

IELTS General Training
Reading 1 Unsolved

SECTION 1

Questions 1–14   **Saturday, 14 January 2017**

Questions 1–6

Look at the advertisements **A–J**.

Answer the questions below by writing the correct letters **A–J** in boxes 1–6 on your answer sheet.

1. Which shoe can be lowered and raised?   A , J

2. Which **TWO** types of casual shoes are sold for children? G , B

3. Which **TWO** types of shoes are suitable for both men and women? E , H

4. Which shoe is shipped from another country?   I

5. Which **TWO** shoes come with additional items at no extra cost? F , G

6. Which **TWO** types of shoes come in only two different colours? G

SHOE WORLD

Family Footwear

A. Outdoors

Summer or winter, our Outdoors range are the best choice to meet your child's schooling requirements. Our shoes feature a comfortable inner sole and easy-tie laces. Only occasional cleaning needed. Shoes come in two sizes. $10 and $20 varieties available.

B. Cool-Clicks

Fashion shoes for children. Open back, great, relaxed summer shoe. Flat-soled, easy to put on and off. One size only, in black or brown – $35.

C. The Pace-Setter

Popular thin-soled men's sports shoe. Double leather surface for greater durability. Trendy and fashionable – half green, half blue with colourful red and yellow stripped laces – $50.

D. Jeansia

Ladies footwear as per the design of a Paris-based boutique fashion house. Winner of 2009 Gloria Award. The shiny silver coating makes the Jeansia even more attractive. Adjustable heels in all sizes – $75.

E. Easy-Wear

A favourite among working men and women. A light-weight, comfortable shoe for daily use. The Rexene surface adds to shoe durability. Variety of embossed icons printed on each pair; choose as per your design taste – $35.

F. Formal

Men's formal shoes. Won silver medal in recent EU Summer Fashion Show. Available in white and brown shades. 3-layer sole, all in beautiful leather. Purchase includes a free shoe brush – $85.

G. Everyday

Cost-effective, everyday children's shoe. Available in a variety of cute, vibrant hues. Animal cartoon prints – cows, donkeys, horses and elephants in greys and whites. Durable rubber sole. One extra pair of laces free – $15.

H. Sunny

Unisex shoes made of pure Italian leather. Two different styles – Hawaii and Malaya. Comfortable walking shoes, great for around the home. Available in brown only, no cleaning needed. Waterproof and come in two styles – $35 and $45.

I. Bosa-Nova

Exceptional country-style women's footwear. The Bosa-Nova is our only imported shoe. The curved sole, actually massages your feet as you walk. Genuine leather upper. Purple-coloured elastic back, a variety of sizes – $95.

J. Supreme

Elegant choice for ladies. Thin but durable leather processed using the latest micro-fibre technology. Will look new for years to come. 4 different colours in 2 sizes. Medium-heel with see-through, flat sole. Stylish black laces. $125.

> **Customers may visit any of our stores and place a personal order. Depending upon stock availability, individual stores periodically offer discounts on particular models. Please note that apart from our discounted shoes, our usual 1-year guarantee applies to all advertised shoes.**

Special 'Festival' offer

$20 gift voucher with every purchase over $100. Valid until the first week of January.

Refund policy

There is no money back for goods purchased unless they have defects. Goods sold and unused may be exchanged for other goods of an equivalent price.

Questions 7–14

The text about **CD Summaries** has eight sections, **A–H.**

Choose the correct heading for sections **A–H** from the CD Directory below.

Write the correct number, **i–xii,** in boxes **7–14** on your answer sheet.

CD Directory – Montreal Public Library

    i. Canada's Forests

   ii. Mountain Biking: Routes in Canada

  iii. Canada Shopping Guide

   iv. Foods: Prepare a Canadian Dish!

    v. Insects of Canada: Visualisation and Illustration

   vi. Private Property: Canada Buying Guide

  vii. Canadian Demography

 viii. 4-Wheel Driving: Canada's Challenge

   ix. Canadian Desert Art

    x. Survival in Canada's Wild

   xi. Canadian Wildlife Cycles

  xii. Food for Thought: Philosophy and Canadian Society

  7. Section **A**

  8. Section **B**

  9. Section **C**

10. Section **D**

11. Section **E**

12. Section **F**

13. Section **G**

14. Section **H**

CD Summaries

A. The driest parts of Canada have a long history of aboriginal people. Among other findings, archaeologists have uncovered evidence of their creativity – ancient painting, pottery and stone-made statues of imaginary characters. This CD contains high resolution images of their creative expression. Some drawings have been reproduced. Extensive photographs and informative texts.

B. This CD is a compilation of information regarding Canada's human populations. In-depth information about population size, growth, density, and distribution are covered. Statistics and graphs presented which bring the information to life! Migration trends in Canada are also a focus. A publication for beginners and experts alike.

C. A manual on Canada's woods and jungles. Satellite images as well as illustrations. Full of useful data. The origins, development and future of landscape trends are discussed. Several case studies on the natural resources in jungles and the impact of industrialisation upon them.

D. Contains a detailed list of Canada's retailers from several industries – souvenirs, fashion, toys, electronics to name a few. A must-have for tourists. Addresses, phone numbers and opening hours are all provided. Relevant internet sites are also easy to access. A world of information is just a click away!

E. If you are a person who thinks that crossing hilly areas on two wheels is the ultimate in excitement then this CD is for you! Contains detailed routes through the slopes of Canada. Full of relevant and useful tips, including how to handle varying weather conditions. Additional information on camping and crisis management also included.

F. Full of authentic Canadian recipes. Lunch, dinner, snacks, ice-creams, deserts and lots more. Select, specialty dishes with some drink preparation tips also included. Some video footage from Canada's top cook shows. Possible purchase locations for some of the rare cooking ingredients, especially spices and natural herbs, are provided.

G. Graphics illustrators have worked with entomologists to give us an idea how these small creatures reproduce and have survived for thousands of years. Their contribution to soil protection is discussed. Pest control and its pros and cons are drawn from articles published by the National University of Canada.

H. Focuses on outdoor safety including infections and self-medications, safety equipment, food, living arrangements and other wildlife skills. Weather changes and ways to cope with them are discussed in detail. A photo gallery featuring a selection of picturesque, natural Canadian scenery is included free with every CD.

Questions 15–27

Read the Text and Answer Questions 15–20.

Mountain Biking?
Canada Is Calling!

Experience the best summer adventure ever!

12 Mountain Biking Adventures Throughout Canada

At Zenith Biking we have been exceeding mountain bikers' expectations since our founding in 1988 in Ottawa, Canada. Over the years we have expanded our operations to cover other Canadian cities including Montreal and Toronto. Currently, with a base of over 100 experienced staff, we are your first choice for mountain biking!

For the past five years our international network, comprising offices in four continents, has been organising Canadian mountain biking adventures for bikers around the world. Annually, an average of 3000 clients enjoy an unforgettable biking experience throughout Canada. Should you be interested in extending your adventure to other countries, our extensive Inter-country Zenith Network can organise additional connections for you. Obtaining a visa for entry into some countries can be a time-consuming and frustrating process however at Zenith, our experienced team will assist you in obtaining your visa least amount of time.

At Zenith we have our own accommodation facilities for bikers, in Ottawa and Toronto. Accommodation fees are reasonable and depend on the size and the location of the room chosen. The most economical option is our 8-bed dorms.

Summer Experience, 2012

Fees for this adventure include:

Return air-ticket from London to Toronto (excluding onward travel in Canada)

➤ Bikers' kit (consisting of apparel, headgear and energy food)

➤ Direct transfer to Meet & Greet camp from airport

➤ Bikers workshop for beginners to advanced by our experienced staff

➤ Extensive directory of Canadian Hills and Mountains

➤ Zenith Biking 24-hour help and support phone service

➤ 24-hour emergency medical assistance.

Eligibility

Participants must:

➤ be at least 18 years old

➤ be in excellent physical condition

➤ have at least a basic level of mountain biking competence

➤ be excited about the experience of a lifetime!

Join the Zenith Bikers' Forum (ZBF)

Once you book with us for any biking experience, you will automatically become a member of the Zenith Bikers' Forum (ZBF). Based on the many requests we received from our clients we formally launched the ZBF 3 years ago. On the ZBF you can ask and have answered any biking-related questions you may have. Our website also has a chat-room. You are encouraged to submit your ideas, questions and suggestions and they will be quickly answered by past clients and staff.

Questions 15–20

Complete the summary below with a word taken from the passage.

Use **NO MORE THAN THREE WORDS AND/OR A NUMBER** for each answer.

Write your answers in boxes 15–20 on your answer sheet.

Zenith Biking began in 1988 in the city of... **Ottawa**... and provides biking adventures in several 15 _Canadian cities_

Experienced Zenith staff provide assistance for bikers worldwide via an 16 _IN netw_. Not all of Zenith's 3000 annual clients mountain bike in Canada – the Inter-country Zenith Network can organise connections to 17 _other countries_.

In Ottawa and Toronto, Zenith Accommodation is available and room rates are based on 18 _the room chooses_. The Summer Experience 2012 offers several exciting options including air-ticket, transport and 24-hour emergency service.

The Zenith Bikers' Forum began 19 _automatically_ and helps paying customers by answering all biking-related questions. Customers can also find answers to their questions in the 20 _2012_ .websites

---

Read the Text and Answer Questions 21–27.

CLASSIFIED ADS – A USEFUL JOB-SEEKING RESOURCE

In their search for employment, increasing numbers of job seekers are once again turning to the help-wanted classified ads in their local newspapers. For some time this popular resource slumped as the heavily trafficked internet job sites became widely regarded as offering greater numbers of employment opportunities. In many cases this is a valid assumption. A local newspaper focuses on positions vacant in a specific town or region, whereas the on-line job site will typically contain advertisements for the whole country and possibly even overseas.

If you are seeking work in your neighbourhood, and do not wish to drive a long distance or move, the local, classified ads in your newspaper may be a viable option. Recent canvassing has revealed that some local and regional employers don't always post their position vacant ads on the major web sites. Many prefer to advertise closer to home and to hire locally in order to avoid having to pay relocation costs.

Often it is not necessary to purchase the newspapers, as these publications are widely available in libraries, coffee shops and even some waiting rooms. In addition, on-line newspaper editions, which contain the help-wanted ads, are now widely available and have contributed to the popularity of this form of advertising. These ads are usually searchable by date, category, keyword and location, making them competitive with the larger career and employment agencies found on the Internet.

Whether you apply for a job through a large, on-line employment agency or via a classified ad in a newspaper the same strategy is valid. First of all, read the ad carefully and do your best to answer the following questions:

Am I the type of person the employer is looking for – do I have the essential skills and experience?

With whom would I be working – a group of people, one person or would I work independently?

What other talents and experience can I include in my application?

What opportunities and experiences might be available in this position that would be advantageous to my career?

Do I have the skills to negotiate the challenges and problems of the position? (For example: working with much older employees or a woman working in an office full of men.)

Importantly, try to find a way to stand out from the other applicants. Remember, whether you are responding to a positions vacant advertisement from an internet agency or a newspaper, your goal is to secure the interview before you stand a chance of being hired for the job.

Questions 21–27

Do the following statements agree with the information given in the text?

In boxes **21–27** on your answer sheet, write

TRUE if the statement agrees with the information

FALSE if the statement contradicts the information

NOT GIVEN if there is no information on this

21. Classified ads have become more popular due to increases in unemployment.

22. On-line job sites list more vacancies than job sites in newspapers. T

23. Internet job sites are recommended for local employment positions. F

24. To avoid paying for moving expenses, employers advertise locally. T

25. Compared with jobs online, jobs in newspapers require a slightly different approach. T

26. An application should mention additional, relevant work experience. T

27. When answering a positions vacant ad, the first aim is to be hired. F

SECTION 3

Read the Passage and Answer questions 28–40.

Issued by the Bank of New South Wales in 1816, Police Fund Notes were one of the first official notes in Australia and were well-circulated throughout the 19th century. Their use continued up until 1910, around which time the Federal Government became responsible for issuing, monitoring and controlling all currencies that were used throughout the country. Once the Australian Notes Act was passed in 1910, it took three years for the Federal Government to issue the first series of Australian notes. The Government followed the British Imperial system where twelve pence made a shilling and twenty shillings made a pound. The same Act also stopped different states and their banks from issuing and circulating their own notes. The status of 'state notes' as legal tender ceased from that time resulting in the Commonwealth Treasury having full responsibility and control over issuing notes. In 1920 however, control was transferred to a Board of Directors directly appointed by the Commonwealth Government.

By the end of 1924 a number of changes took place regarding the control of note issuing, the most significant being the replacement of the Commonwealth Government Board of Directors by the Commonwealth Bank Board of Directors. Gradually, the Commonwealth Bank became the sole authority to issue Australian notes. This authority was formalised in 1945 by the Commonwealth Bank Act. In 1960, control was passed to another authority, the Reserve Bank of Australia (RBA), which took over the responsibility of central banking and the issuing of notes. In 1966 the RBA converted its currency from the Imperial system to decimal currency and named its standard currency the dollar.

In the 1970's Australia experienced rapid growth in its economy and population. This growth meant that more currency would need to be printed so the RBA began the construction of a new note printing complex in Melbourne. In 1981, the first batch of notes was printed in the new complex by the printing branch of the RBA which, in 1990, was officially named Note Printing Australia. In addition to larger-scale note printing, the RBA also concentrated on developing technologically advanced and complex note printing mechanisms to guard against counterfeiting. As a result of joint efforts by the RBA and the

Commonwealth Scientific and Industrial Research Organisation (CSIRO), revolutionary polymer notes were invented. Featuring exclusively a pictorial theme of settlement incorporating elements of Aboriginal culture, commemorative $10 polymer notes were introduced in 1988 as part of Australia's bi-centennial celebrations.

The basic idea of developing polymer notes originated from an experiment where the RBA attempted to insert an Optically Variable Device (OVD) in the notes so that counterfeiters could not copy them. Over the years, a process has evolved in the production of polymer note printing which involves several steps. Initially, blank sheets are made out of a special kind of surface material called Biaxially Oriented Polypropylene (BOPP) – a non-fibrous and non-porous polymer used as an alternative to paper in note printing that has a distinctive feel when touched. Usually, a technique called Opacifying is then used to apply ink to each side of the sheet through a die-cut that has a sealed space in it for the OVD – no ink is placed in this area, it remains transparent. The sheet is then ready for Intaglio Printing, a kind of printing which sets the ink in an embossed form, raising the printed elements – text, image, lines and other complicated shapes. The process then prints a see-through registration device by matching the images on both sides, dot by dot. If the images on both sides do not align perfectly, then the see-through device will not show any printing on it once the note is held up to a light source. As a special security feature, Shadow Image Creation technique is then used by applying Optically Variable Ink (OVI) which allows the print on the reverse side to be also seen. All the notes then undergo a safety and functionality test where they are placed in front of a light source to check manually whether or not the reverse side can be seen. If the notes pass the test, it is assumed that the process has been successful.

The process then moves to Micro Printing, which is the printing of text so small that it can only be read with a magnifying glass. The second last phase of the process is Florescence Printing where some texts are printed in such a way that is only visible when viewed under ultra-violet (UV) light. The authenticity of a polymer note can be quickly established by holding it up to a UV light source – if some texts glow under the UV light then the note is authentic. The last phase of the process is called varnishing, which is the over-coating of notes with a chemical that consists of drying oil, resin and thinner. This final phase makes the surfaces of the notes glossy and more durable.

Despite significant developments of technology and control, some people argue that the life of polymer notes as currency in Australia will come to an end due to the widespread usage of electronic fund transfer cards[1]. Whether this will come to pass remains to be seen. One thing however seems certain, innovation of currency notes in Australia will continue into the foreseeable future.

Questions 28–34

Complete the flowchart below.

Choose **NO MORE THAN TWO WORDS** from the text for each answer.

Write your answers in boxes **28–34** on your answer sheet.

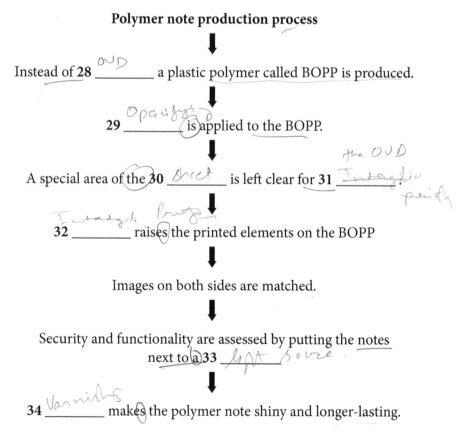

Polymer note production process

↓

Instead of **28** _____ a plastic polymer called BOPP is produced.

↓

29 _____ is applied to the BOPP.

↓

A special area of the **30** _____ is left clear for **31** _____

↓

32 _____ raises the printed elements on the BOPP

↓

Images on both sides are matched.

↓

Security and functionality are assessed by putting the notes next to a **33** _____

↓

34 _____ makes the polymer note shiny and longer-lasting.

---

[1] Computer-based systems used to perform financial transactions electronically without physically exchanging notes or coins.

Questions 35–39

Do the following statements agree with the information given in the text?

In boxes **35–40** on your answer sheet, write

TRUE if the statement agrees with the information

FALSE if the statement contradicts the information

NOT GIVEN if there is no information on this

35. Police Fund Notes were the first and only notes used in Australia. F

36. The first notes issued by the Bank of New South Wales followed the British Imperial System. T

37. The first series of Australian notes were released in 1910. F

38. The construction of the note printing complex in Melbourne was due to economic progress in Australia. T

39. Illustrations on the first Australian polymer note featured Australia's bi-centenary. N G

Question 40

Choose the correct question, **A–E.**

Write the correct letter in **box 40** on your answer sheet.

Which of the following is the most suitable title for **Section 3?**

A. Early Australian money

B. The economy of Australia

C. New polymer notes for Australia

D. Changes in Australian money

E. The future of Australian money

Answers

1. **D** It is mentioned that Jeansia shoes have adjustable heels, which means the height of the shoes can be lowered or raised.

2. **B, G** It is mentioned that Cool-Clicks are fashion shoes for children, open back, relaxed summer shoe. Also, Everyday shoes are cost-effective everyday shoes (i.e. casual shoes) for kids.

3. **E, H** It is mentioned that Easy-Wear shoes are for both men and women. Sunny shoes are unisex shoes, which means these are for both men and women.

4. **I** It is mentioned that Bosa-Nova is the only imported shoe. Imported means that it is brought/shipped from another country.

5. **F, G** It is mentioned that Formal shoes come with a free shoe brush. Everyday shoes come with one pair of free laces.

6. **B, F** It is mentioned that Cool-Clicks come in Black and Brown and Formal shoes come in White and Brown shades (i.e. colours).

7. **ix** CD ix mentions art, which relates to creativity. It also mentions deserts, which refers to the driest parts of Canada.

8. **vii** Demography for a country refers to the population size, growth, density, etc.

9. **i** Canada's Forest can contain information about Canada's woods and jungles.

10. **iii** Shopping guide contains information regarding shops, items sold, opening times etc.

11. **ii** Crossing hilly areas in two wheels refers to mountain biking.

12. **iv** Preparing Canadian dishes refer to Canadian recipes.

13. **v** Entomology refers to the study of insects. 'Small creatures' and 'pests' are used to describe insects.

14. **x** Outdoor safety, food, self-medication, wild living etc. refer to survival techniques in wildlife as it throws lot of challenges to the travellers.

Lab 3, Reading Passage 2, Answers and Suggestions

Quest. Number Answer Scott's Tips for Answering the Questions

15. Canadian cities. It is mentioned that Zenith operates in several Canadian cities.

16. International network. It is mentioned that Zenith serves bikers from around the world via an international network.

17. Other countries. It is mentioned that Zenith can make connections to other countries for the bikers through its Inter-country Network.

18. Size and location. It is mentioned that room rates depend on the size and location of the room chosen.

19. 3 years ago. It is mentioned that ZBF started operating 3 years ago.

20. Chat-room. It is specified that customers can also get their questions answered in the chat-room.

21. **Not Given** There is nothing in the passage about this! There is a statement that looking for ads in local newspapers is increasing but nothing is mentioned about why.

22. **True** The first paragraph states, "For some time this popular resource (newspaper ads) slumped as the heavily trafficked internet job sites became widely regarded as offering greater numbers of employment opportunities."

   This means that there were more online job ads than those listed in newspapers.

23. **False** The first and second paragraphs state: "on-line job sites will typically contain advertisements for the whole country and possibly even overseas... If you are seeking work in your neighborhood...the local, classified ads in your newspaper may be a viable option."

   This means online jobs cover a larger area (whole country and overseas) while local ads are for local jobs.

24. **True** The second paragraph states: "Many (employers) prefer to advertise closer to home and to hire locally in order to avoid paying relocation costs."

25. **False** The third paragraph states: "Whether you apply for a job through a large, on-line employment agency or via a classified ad in a newspaper the same strategy is valid."

   This means the application process is the same.

26. **True** The passage states: Do your best to answer the following questions... " What other talents and experience can I include in my application?"

   In other words, a person applying for a job should aim to include relevant experience with their application.✓

27. **False** The final paragraph states: "...your goal is to secure the interview before you stand a chance of being hired for the job."

   This means the first aim is to secure an interview and then be hired for the job.

Lab 3, Reading Passage 3: Answers and Suggestions

Quest. Number Answer Scott's Tips for Answering the Questions

28. **paper** It is mentioned that BOPP is used as an alternate to (i.e. instead of) paper.

29. **ink** It is mentioned that ink is applied on each side of the BOPP sheet.

30. **sheet**

   OR

   BOPP It is mentioned that a part of the sheet (which is made of BOPP) is left transparent (i.e. there is no ink, which means it is left clear).

31. **OVD** The process mentions that the sealed space is left for OVD.

32. **Intaglio Printing** It is mentioned that Intaglio Printing sets the ink in an embossed form that raises the printed elements.

33. **light source** It is mentioned that by placing (i.e. putting) the notes in front of a light source the security (i.e. safety) and functionality are tested.

34. **varnishing** The process mentions about varnishing, which is applying chemical to make the notes glossy (i.e. shiny) and durable (i.e. longer-lasting).

35. **False** The passage mentions that Police Fund Notes were one of the first official notes, which means these were not the only notes.

36. **Not Given** It is mentioned that the notes issued by the Government followed the British system. Whether the notes issued by the Bank of New South Wales also had followed that system or not is not given.

37. **False** It is mentioned that it took three years to release the first series of Australian notes once the Act was passed in 1910. This means that the notes were released not in 1910 but in 1913.

38. **True** It is mentioned that the new note printing complex was due to Australia's rapid growth in economy and population. Economic growth refers to economic progress.

39. **False** It is mentioned that the first Polymer note featured exclusively a theme (which means the only theme) of settlement and elements of Aboriginal culture. The notes were launched on the occasion of Australia's bi-centenary but did not feature anything regarding it, as the only theme was settlement.

40. **D** The passage discusses the changes in Australian money that took place over the years – the changes of authority to issue money, the changes in materials used to print money and the changes in circulation of money.

IELTS General Training Reading 2

SECTION 1

Questions 1–14

Read the text and answer Questions 1–7.

UTOPIAN ISLAND TOURS

ISLAND OVERVIEW AND BOOKINGS

As New Zealand's most attractive tour company, Utopian Island Tours is always there for you to make your trip to Waki Island enjoyable.

Making a Booking

Bookings require three forms of identification. This means you should provide us with a document showing your residential address, your passport (if not NZ citizen) and a phone number where you can be contacted. You can log on to our website and fill in the online booking form, you can call 425 125 483 or you can visit us in person at any of our 3 booking centres at Customs Road, City Centre and South Queens Road.

Departure Times and Rates for Our Tours

Single Day Tours

Monday to Thursday: Depart 11.00 a.m., arrive 7.00 p.m.

Friday to Sunday: Depart 8.45 a.m., arrival 9.00 p.m.

Rates – Single: $150, Couple: $250, Child under 12: $50

Two-day Tours

Monday to Thursday: Depart 11.00 a.m., arrive 5.30 p.m. (2 days later)

Friday to Sunday: Depart 8.45 a.m., arrive 9.00 p.m. (2 days later)

Rates – Single: $250, Couple: $400, Child under 12: $90

Things to Bring

- ➤ Warm clothes, weather can be quite unpredictable.
- ➤ Camera with reels, if SLR. The only photo studio at Waki often runs short of film.
- ➤ Binoculars can be great – you may spot some wildlife!
- ➤ Fishing gear.
- ➤ 2-day tourists like to bring their favourite drinks for the traditional first night BBQ.

Entertainment Options Available On the Island

Bars

Waki has three bars, all by the sea that remain open till late.

Shopping

Waki has a native handicraft bazaar right in the city centre. With all items reasonably priced, the bazaar is a fantastic place for souvenir hunters!

Restaurants

A variety of restaurants specialising in Waki sea-food are in demand on the island. A selection of other restaurants from hamburgers to Asian cuisine is also available.

Vineyard

Waki Island summer wines are reaching as far as Europe and US. Come and sample the delicious Waki wines!

Cancellations

In order to receive a full refund, cancellations must be made at least 7 days prior to the departure date. Cancellations made 1 to 6 days prior to departure will receive a partial refund of up to 50%. Cancellations made on the departure date will not be given a refund.

Questions 1–7

Do the following statements agree with the information given in the text?

In boxes **1–7** on your answer sheet, write

TRUE if the statement agrees with the information

FALSE if the statement contradicts the information

NOT GIVEN if there is no information on this

1. New Zealand citizens must bring their passports to book a Utopian Island tour.

2. Tours can be booked on the Internet.

3. Larger groups (over 10) may receive a discount.

4. Two-day tours leaving on Wednesday arrive later than two-day tours that leave on Sunday.

5. The climate on Waki Island often changes.

6. All the bars on Waki Island are next to the ocean.

7. A person cancelling a trip one week before the departure date will receive a 100% refund.

Read the Advertisements for Apartments Below and Answer Questions 8–14

Rental Apartment Ads

A. Northland Apartments
Modern two bedroom, two bathroom dwellings with security parking for one car. Kitchen/Dining area, fully furnished. Each apartment is part of a three-story boutique-style building. Sea views on one side. One garden courtyard. Rent $1400 per month. Two month's rental bond required. Inspection is available only on weekends by appointment.

Notes	
Positives	**Negatives**
• stunning modern architecture, award winning boutique building • furniture and fixtures almost new • close to the beach, restaurants and pubs • heated swimming pool • pool and garden maintained by estate agent • one tennis court within the complex • 24-hour security camera.	• no lift facility, stairs only • maintenance fee of $500 for swimming pool, tennis court and security system • utility bills must be paid separately • minimum two months' notice required before leaving • noisy during summer in the beach area • no intercom facility.

B. Peninsula Apartments
Fully furnished, one bedroom apartment in a spacious complex. One bathroom and large kitchen counters. Security guards on patrol 24 hours a day. Located in the heart of the City Shopping Complex area. Commercial establishments are located from the ground to the 7th floors with one-bedroom apartments on floors 8 to 12. Rent $900 per month, no rental bond required but one referral is mandatory.

Notes	
Positives	**Negatives**
• roof top BBQ and party area • free membership at the Wellbeing Gym, (normally $100 per month) • all interior fittings are imported from Italy • separate lifts available from the ground floor directly to the apartment floors.	• no reserved parking for apartment tenants – tenants need to park in public parking or in the shopping complex parking next door • apartments have no windows – natural outdoor ventilation comes via the corridor outside each apartment • electricity, gas and water bills separate.

C. Mascot Apartments

Spaciously planned, open studio apartments at the posh residential area of Endeavour Hill. Separate bathroom and toilet – German fittings. Rent per month $1200. One month's rental bond required. All apartments come with a balcony and windows on two sides. One garage per apartment.

Notes	
Positives	**Negatives**
• separate guest entertainment lounge at each floor • central air-conditioning and heating installed • high speed broadband internet pre-installed, added $40 per month required • free window and carpet cleaning every three months.	• no nearby public transport, although taxi stand is close • nearest train station is a 25-minute walk • 25 year old building • no guest parking on premises • apartments not furnished.

D. Villa Apartments

Three bedrooms, two bathrooms, two parking and one large living room. Separate kitchen. Fully furnished. Rent $2000 per month, all bills payable separately. Ideal for a family of 4. Lift as well as stair access to each floor. 24-hour alarm and security cameras. Two grocery shops, one convenience store and one saloon on the ground floor. No rental bond required. One month notice essential.

Notes	
Positives	**Negatives**
• new building and furniture – built in 2005	• domestic airport and major highway nearby
• close to Custom Street ferry terminal – charming outdoor walk and entertainment areas	• heavy traffic during weekday peak hours is to be expected
• open roof area for small-scale parties	• restricted speed limits due to school next door.
• kids' playground on the 1st floor	
• next to train station, bus stop and local school	
• guest parking facilities.	

Questions 8–14

Look at the *four advertisements,* **A–D.**

For which apartment are the following statements true?

Write the correct letter, **A, B, C or D,** in boxes **8–14** on your answer sheet.

8. This apartment would suitable for a family with children.

9. A recommendation from somebody else is a must before renting this apartment.

10. Surrounding areas would NOT be quiet during the warmest time of the year.

11. People with their own furniture would consider this accommodation.

12. This apartment would not be a good choice for people who have difficulty walking.

13. Pre-rental viewing is possible only on fixed days.

14. A local fitness centre will not charge residents of these apartments anything for membership.

SECTION 2

Questions 15–27

Read the information below and answer Questions 15–21.

CMG Bank

Credit Card Contract Information

Dear Customer,

Thank you for applying for a CMG Bank Credit Card.

A *Credit Card Contract* between you (the Primary Card Holder) and CMG Bank will govern the usage of your Credit Card. Please take the time to read and understand the following information, which is an overview of the important parts of our contract with you, our valued customer.

Identification

It is a requirement that you provide CMG verification of your identity. This is a legal requirement which can be met by producing any two of the following documents:

    A. Driver's Licence

    B. Birth Certificate

    C. Valid Passport

    D. Any existing Credit Card details

At least one of the above documents MUST contain your photograph and signature.

Credit Limit

The credit limit you are entitled to will be provided in the Letter of Offer, which you will receive if your application is successful. You may request an increase in your credit limit at any time. The bank reviews all requests and usually notifies customers after five (5) working days.

You must not exceed your credit limit unless CMG Bank has authorised you to do so in writing. If you exceed your limit, a warning letter and/or email is sent to you and a penalty fee of £40 will be automatically debited from your account. Funds exceeding your limit are also charged at the highest rate of interest (check www.cmgbank. co.uk for updated rates).

Rules for Use

- ➤ CMG Bank Credit Card must be used wholly and exclusively by you and/or nominated user(s).

- ➤ Use of the card for any unlawful purposes (i.e. purchase of goods or services that are prohibited by law) will result in immediate suspension.

- ➤ If you require a card for exclusive business use, please telephone a local CMG branch and ask about Business Credit Card.

Additional Cards

- ➤ You can nominate any person over 16 to be a Secondary User. This means they can carry an additional card that will be linked to your credit account.

- ➤ You will be responsible and liable for any purchase made on this additional card. It is also your responsibility make available a copy of this contract and explain the Terms and Conditions to any nominated Secondary User. The additional cardholder may make full use of the credit card to purchase goods and services and receive cash advances. Nominated Secondary Users may not request a credit limit increase.

- ➤ Once you have nominated a Secondary User, CMG will mail the additional card to the person. Please make sure you provide the correct address.

- ➤ The primary card holder is able to cancel an additional card at any time by filling a from at our Card Cancellation Department.

(continued)

Purchasing from Merchants

➤ A CMG Bank Credit Card is accepted by all merchants displaying the card symbol.

➤ The price a merchant charges for goods and/or services purchased may differ from a cash price. CMG will not bear any liability for merchants' pricing.

➤ If you have a complaint regarding goods or services purchased, you need to resolve the issue with the merchant directly.

Questions 15–18

Do the following statements agree with the information given in the passage?

In boxes **15–18** on your answer sheet, write

TRUE if the statement agrees with the information

FALSE if the statement contradicts the information

NOT GIVEN if there is no information on this

15. The maximum amount of money a customer can spend is stated in the Letter of Offer.

16. If a customer exceeds their credit limit, interest and £40 will be charged.

17. The CMG Bank Credit Card may also be used for some business transactions.

18. Secondary users will be responsible for any purchase they make.

Questions 19–21

Complete the sentences below with words taken from the passage.

Use **NO MORE THAN THREE WORDS** for each answer.

Write your answers in boxes **19–21** on your answer sheet.

19. Out of four verification documents, one must have the applicant's _____.

20. CMG's response to requests for a credit limit increase takes _____.

21. Clients wanting a _____should phone the bank.

Read the Text and Answer Questions 22–27.

CMG Bank

Card Descriptions and Options

CMG Silver Card

Enjoy a low annual fee as well as a low 7% per annum interest on purchases. Cash advances must be requested in writing. The Silver Card offers customers a credit limit of up to £2000 which makes it a great card for junior executives and people in casual employment. Apply on or before July 15 for the special promotional offer – 55 days interest free* purchase. A fixed annual fee of only £45 or £30 if you are currently a CMG banking customer.

CMG Gold Card

A low 9% interest rate per annum with a credit limit of up to £3000. Automatic cash advance facilities**. An annual fee of only £50 if customers link their credit account with their existing CMG savings account. For non-CMG customers, the annual fee is £65. Special Gold-Class online protection for internet transactions. Upon request, phone banking facilities are activated for fund transfers. Optional insurance cover for loss or theft of the card – a standard fee of £40 annually applies for this option.

CMG Gold *Plus* Card

Become a Gold Plus Card holder before July 31 and enjoy no interest and no repayments for 3 months! Earn bonus points for every purchase. Earn cash or airline ticket rewards for accumulated points – one point for every dollar spent***. A credit limit of £5000 applies with an interest free period of 45 days. Annual fee of £75. Three Secondary User cards at no additional issuing cost which incur a low annual fee of £10 per card.

(continued)

CMG Platinum Card

If you apply online before August 31 during our special promotional period, you will enjoy no interest charges for up to 6 months. Always 55 days interest free credit on all purchases. A credit limit of up to £7,500 available upon request. The Platinum Card has been specially designed for managers and high level executives. An annual fee of £100 applies. Year-end inter-state airline ticket gift for all cardholders in good standing. Five Secondary User cards may be issued at no extra cost. 2 points for every dollar spent in the rewards programme. Rewards include: home furniture, electronic goods, free petrol, kitchen appliances, clothing and more!

Additional Optional Services

CMG Credit Cover (CCC)

CCC is an option customers may choose that helps to provide peace of mind. If you experience an illness or injury or become involuntarily unemployed, CCC insures that your minimum monthly credit payment will be met. In the event of your total and permanent disablement, CCC will pay your credit card balance in full. CCC covers any loss due to stolen cards.

Security Plus

Protects you against any fraudulent use of your credit card and other valuable personal possessions like mobile phones and laptop computers. It is an outsourced service from Secure Plus Insurance Company Ltd. that works in close association with CMG. For a nominal yearly cost of £25 you can enjoy the benefits of this service. Simply register the details of your card(s) and valuables with Security Plus. If your card(s) or other possessions are lost or stolen, inform Security Plus. Your accounts will be blocked and measures will be taken to recover your items.

* *does not apply to cash advances*

** *an interest rate of 17% applies to cash advances*

*** *no points are awarded for cash advances*

Questions 22–27

Choose the correct letter, **A, B, C or D.**

Write your answers in boxes **22–27** on your answer sheet.

22. The CMG Silver Card

    A. permits customers to spend up to £2000.

    B. is only for junior executives or casual workers.

    C. must be used on or before July 15.

    D. has a standard fee for all customers.

23. The CMG Gold Card

    A. provides internet security.

    B. offers free insurance against theft.

    C. provides a selection of insurers.

    D. requires cardholders to have a CMG savings account

24. The CMG Gold Plus Card

    A. allows for additional cards at no extra cost.

    B. allows owners to spend more than £5000 interest free.

    C. offers a reward for each dollar spent.

    D. is offering a special deal for new customers.

25. The CMG Platinum Card

    A. does not charge interest for a period of 6 months.

    B. costs £100 per year.

    C. automatically offers customers a £7,500 credit limit.

    D. offers an automatic credit limit of £15,000.

26. Security Plus

    A. is a service that operates through mobile phones.

    B. is a company owned by CMG Bank.

C. prevents the risk of excess funds being transferred by a cardholder.

D. costs £25 per year.

27. **A New Customer not Wanting to Pay High Annual Fees Should Choose the**

    A. CMG Gold Plus Card.

    B. CMG Platinum Card.

    C. CMG Silver Card.

    D. CMG Gold Card.

SECTION 3

Questions 28–40

Read the Passage and Answer Questions 28–40.

Measuring Intelligence

A. Intelligence has been defined as 'a property of mind that enables us to perform a wide variety of mental activities that include reasoning, planning, solving problems and learning new things.' However, psychologists that focus on ways to measure intelligence define it as 'the degree to which one can adapt to one's environment.'

B. The first attempts in the modern era to systematically measure intelligence date back to the beginning of the 20th century. French psychologist Alfred Binet published the first modern intelligence test, the *Binet-Simon intelligence scale* in 1905. His original intention was to identify students that needed extra academic support. Unfortunately, he was not able to complete his work, managing just two revisions of his initial study before he passed away in 1911 at the age of 54.

C. Englishman Sir Francis Galton also contributed to the development of intelligence measurement techniques. His research focused on a slightly different aspect of intelligence that he called *psychometrics*. This area of study was concerned with the measurement of knowledge, abilities, attitudes, and personality traits. Like Binet, he also started his research by focusing on the differences between individuals and groups of individuals. Galton studied people's 'everyday activities' for several weeks and noted that although the activities are common to all people, there were considerable variations in terms of the mental processes required to perform the tasks. Galton's psychometric point of view and Binet's idea of a scale-based measurement of intelligence opened new avenues for further research and inspired other psychologists.

D. The next significant step along the road to measuring intelligence was in 1912 through the work of William Stern. Although Stern did not follow directly on from Binet's work, his research popularised the term *intelligence quotient* or *IQ.* It was Stanford University psychologist Lewis Terman who did continue Binet's work showing, through the *Stanford-Binet Intelligence Scale,* that IQ could be measured. Almost a century later, one of the most effective measurement tools of human intelligence is based upon Stern's original IQ test. Later, in 1906 while at Stanford, Terman published a revised and perfected Binet-Simon scale for American populations. This *Stanford Revision of the Binet-Simon Scale,* soon became known as the *Stanford-Binet,* was considered to be the best available individual intelligence test of its day. Terman's work focused on the scientific diagnosis and classification of children based on their intelligence. Terman followed Stern's research methods and measured human intelligence through use of a formula – the ratio of mental age and chronological age multiplied by 100. Terman's research enabled schools to organise special classes for the students with a low score on the intelligence scale and to develop an advanced curriculum for students who were of superior intelligence. From 1949 to 1955, psychologist David Wechsler developed an integrated intelligence measurement tool. This tool was used to measure the intelligence of both adults and children. Wechsler's tests have grown in popularity amongst today's psychologists with the *Wechsler Adult Intelligence Scale* and *Wechsler Intelligence Scale for Children* being commonly used for adults and children alike.

E. Like all revolutionary inventions, the measurement of IQ also went through a lot of changes during the early phases of its development. Gradually, the complex testing format was simplified and standardised. During the 1990s, IQ measurement was reduced to simply answering some questions in a 30-minute test. IQ measurement systems have proven to be so popular that organisations, clubs and societies have formed which only accept members with certain IQ levels. The most well-known of these groups, *Mensa International,* was founded by an Australian barrister Roland Berrill after he received financial assistance from British technologist, Dr. Lancelot Ware. *Mensa* only accepts members who have scored in the top 2% of a standardised IQ test. Gradually a number of similar clubs and societies have formed worldwide, many of them now well-established authorities that promote human intelligence studies for the benefit of greater humanity.

F. In the present day, psychologists have grouped IQ test forms based on the precise aspects of intelligence to be tested. These IQ tests are usually a mix of problems aimed at measuring short-term memory, pinpointing verbal knowledge, exploring spatial visualisation and calculating the speed of perception. Based upon the method used, some tests have a total time limit while others have a specific time limit for each subset. When it comes to measuring high intelligence however, tests are neither bound by time nor by supervision.

G. The acceptance of modern IQ testing systems increased when the Guinness Book of World Records added a category which they called 'Highest IQ.' Many were surprised to learn that Marilyn Savant, the one given the title, was a university drop-out. There are, however, groups of people who oppose the concept of measuring intelligence. They represent a school of thought that conclude that intelligence is something too abstract to measure and to express in terms of numeric values. It is believed that the development of computer technology will someday resolve the controversies surrounding how intelligence is measured.

Questions 28–34

Look at the following statements (**Questions 28–34**) and the list of people below.

Match each statement with the person to whom it refers.

Write your answers **A–H** in boxes **28–34** on your answer sheet.

28. the foundation for one of the best present-day intelligence measurement tools

29. intellectual ability to do daily work varies from person to person

30. a wealthy man who helped someone to implement an idea

31. the pioneer of contemporary intelligence testing

32. highly intelligent but did not complete university

33. invented a mathematical rule to measure intelligence

34. originated the concept of a group that only accepts members who have high IQs

List of People

A. Lewis Terman

B. Marilyn Savant

C. William Stern

D. Roland Berrill

E. Francis Galton

F. Alfred Binet

G. David Wechsler

H. Lancelot Ware

Questions 35–40

Do the following statements agree with the information given in the text?

In boxes 35–40 on your answer sheet, write

TRUE if the statement agrees with the information

FALSE if the statement contradicts the information

NOT GIVEN if there is no information on this

35. Psychologists that measure intelligence define it as being how easily people can change to suit their surroundings.

36. Binet studied intelligence in order to locate students with learning problems.

37. Galton's research showed that regular human activities use different parts of the brain.

38. Stern's IQ test is considered the best intelligence measurement tool today.

39. IQ tests must be supervised by a qualified professional.

40. Computers are expected to solve the problems related to the measurement of IQ.

Answers

1. **False** It is mentioned that passport is need if the tourist is not New Zealand citizen. This means that New Zealand citizens do not need to bring passport.

2. **True** It is mentioned that one can log on to website and fill in the online booking form. It means that the tours can be booked online.

3. **Not Given** The passage does not specify anything regarding discounts for larger groups.

4. **False** It is mentioned that tours leaving on Wednesday arrive at 5.30 p.m., while tours leaving on Sunday arrive at 9.00 p.m. So, Wednesday tours do not arrive later than Sunday tours, rather they arrive 3 and half hour earlier.

5. **True** It is mentioned that the weather can be quite unpredictable, which means it changes frequently.

6. **True** It is mentioned that the bars are by the sea, which means next to the ocean.

7. **True** It is stated that in order to receive a full refund (i.e. 100% refund), cancellations must be made at least 7 days (i.e. 1 week) prior to the departure date.

8. **D** It is mentioned that it is ideal for family of 4. Family of 4 refers to family with children.

9. **B** It is mentioned that referral is mandatory. Referral means recommendation by somebody and mandatory means that it is a must.

10. **A** It is mentioned that 'the area is noisy during summer.' Noisy means it is loud. Summer is the warmest time of the year.

11. **C** The advertisement clearly states that Mascot Apartments are not furnished.

12. **A** It is mentioned that there is no lift, only stairs. It is not a good choice for people who have difficulty walking (climbing the stairs).

13. **A** It is stated that inspection open only during weekends. Inspection refers to assessment and only during weekend means there are fixed days for inspection.

14. B It is mentioned that the commercial gym (i.e. fitness centre) offers free membership to the tenants. Free membership means there is no charge applicable.

Lab 4, Reading Passage 2: Answers and Suggestions

Quest. Number Answer Scott's Tips for Answering the Questions

15. True It is mentioned that the Letter of Offer mentions the credit limit, which means the maximum amount of money a user can spend.

16. True It is mentioned that a penalty fee of £40 will be changed for exceeding credit limit. It is also mentioned that funds exceeding credit limit will be charged at the highest interest rate.

17. Not Given It is mentioned that clients can get CMG Business Credit Card for dedicated business purposes. But, whether or not the CMG Bank Credit card can be used for some business transaction is not given.

18. False It is mentioned that the primary cardholder will be responsible for any purchase that the secondary users make.

19. Signature and photograph. It is mentioned that among the four documents at least one must have photograph and signature of the applicant.

20. Five working days. It is mentioned that the bank reviews requests for increasing credit limits and notifies within 5 working days.

21. Business Credit Card. It is mentioned that clients looking for a card for business purpose should contact the bank for Business Credit Card.

22. A It is mentioned that the CMG Silver Card has a credit limit of $2000, which means that it permits the user to spend up to $2000.

23. A It is mentioned that CMG Gold Card offers online protection, which means internet security.

24. D If customers become CMG Gold Plus Card holders before July 31 they will enjoy no interest and no repayments for 3 months – this is a special offer.

25. **B** It is mentioned that CMG Platinum Card has an annual fee of £100, which means it costs £100 per year.

26. **D** It is mentioned that Security Plus costs a nominal fee of £25 per year.

27. **C** It can be calculated that for CMG Silver Card the annual fee for a new customer is £45, which is the lowest.

Lab 4, Reading Passage 3: Answers and Suggestions

Quest. Number Answer Scott's Tips for Answering the Questions

28. **C** It is mentioned in Section D that almost a century later, William Stern's test is still considered as the basis (i.e. foundation) for one of the most effective measurement tools of human intelligence.

29. **E** It is mentioned in Section C that Francis Galton studied people's everyday activities (i.e. daily works) and noted considerable variations in terms of the mental (intellectual) processes to perform tasks.

30. **H** It is mentioned in Section E that Lancelot Ware was an affluent (i.e. wealthy) professional who financially helped Berrill to implement the idea of forming a club.

31. **F** It is mentioned in Section B that Alfred Binet published the first (i.e. pioneer) modern (i.e. contemporary) intelligence test.

32. **B** It is mentioned in Section G that Marilyn Savant, a university drop-out (i.e. did not continue study) had the highest IQ in the world.

33. **A** It is stated in Section D that Terman developed a formula (i.e. mathematical rule) to measure intelligence.

34. **D** It is mentioned that in Section E that Roland Berrill started Mensa International that accepted the top 2% IQ scorers as members.

35. **True** It is mentioned that psychologists define intelligence as 'the degree to which one can adapt to one's environment,' which means people's ability to change (adapt) to suit their surroundings (i.e. environment).

36. **True** Section B mentions that Binet's intention of developing intelligence test was to identify (i.e. locate) students that needed extra academic support, which means the students who had learning problems.

37. **Not Given** Section C mentions about Galton's work on individuals and groups of individuals but it does not mention whether or not his research showed that regular human activities use different parts of the brain.

38. **Not Given** Section D mentions that almost a century later, one of the most effective measurement tools of human intelligence is based upon Stern's original IQ test. It does not mention that Stern's test is the best. Also, 'based upon' does not mean that Stern's test is the tool. The answer is not given.

39. **False** Section F mentions that high intelligence tests are not bound by supervision, which means supervision is not mandatory (i.e. a must) for all tests.

40. **True** Section G mentions that someday computers will resolve the controversies (i.e. problems) on how intelligence is measured.

LISTENING TEST

FORMAT

➤ This module lasts about 30 minutes long.

➤ At the end of the test, candidates are given 10 minutes to transfer their answers to the answer sheet.

➤ This module is same for both the academic and general students.

➤ There are total 4 sections with 10 questions in each section carrying 1 mark.

SECTIONS DIVISION

The four sections named A B C and D are of following types

A. It is a conversation between two people set in everyday social situations.

B. It is a monologue set in everyday social situations.

C. It is a conversation between three to four people set in an educational background or training context.

D. It is a monologue on an academic subject.

TYPES

➤ Fill Ups

➤ Match the following

➤ Multiple Choice Questions (MCQs)

TIPS

➢ Always read the questions when you are given time to do so. It will make you familiar with the questions.

➢ In the last 10 minutes given to you, make sure to check all the spellings and the grammatical forms of the answers that you are transferring.

➢ Try to match the keywords from the questions to the speaker's words, they do not always use the same vocabulary as written. Try to understand the context of the conversation and then mark out the synonyms.

➢ If you miss a question, don't waste your time on it because you may miss the answer to the next one. So, if you miss one, move on.

➢ Always make sure to follow the word count given in the instructions.

➢ Always cross check your answers from your answer sheet to your listening booklet.

Solved Examples

➢ MCQ's

Choose the correct answer, A, B or C.

1. Dave Hadley says that the computer system has

    A. too many users.

    B. never worked well.

    C. become outdated.

2. The main problem with the computer system is that it

    A. is too slow

    B. stops working

    C. displays incorrect data

3. Timetabling has become an issue because

    A. there is not enough time for anyone to do it.

    B. the system does not handle course options.

    C. the courses are constantly changing.

4. To solve the timetabling issues, Randhir suggests that

    A. students should create their own timetables

    B. Dave should have someone to assist him.

    C. the number of courses should be reduced.

5. Randhir says that a new system may

    A. need to be trialled.

    B. still have problems

    C. be more economical

6. Improving the existing system will take

    A. a few weeks.

    B. four or five months.

    C. nine months

Answers

1. C	**4.** A
2. A	**5.** C
3. B	**6.** B

Transcripts

Randhir: Hello, I'm Randhir from the Technologies department.

Dave: Ah yes. Good. I'm Dave. Thanks for coming to see me. I'm responsible for student admissions to the college and I use a computer system to help process student enrolments and to do the timetabling. But it really doesn't suit the way we work these days. **It's over ten years old** and although it was fine when it was first introduced. **It's just not good enough now.**

> So the answer of our first question is C (it has become outdated or old).

Randhir: okay, what problems are you experiencing?

Dave: well, 20 years ago, the college was quite small and we didn't have the numbers of students and teachers that we have now.

Randhir: so, the system can't handle the increasing volumes…

Dave: well, there's lot more data now and it sometimes seems the system has crashed but, in fact, it just **takes ages to go from one screen to the next.**

> Note that the answer while listening could seem like option B, but afterwards, as he says it takes ages, the option is clearly A with computers being slow.

Randhir: is that the only problem?

Dave: well that's the main one, but there are others. In the past, doing the timetabling was quite simple but now we have a lot more courses and what's made it more complicated is that **many of them have options.**

Randhir: right – but the **system should allow you to include those.**

Dave: well, no it doesn't. and I've been given extra responsibility of making the time table as well. If you could do anything to make the process more efficient?

> ➤ In question 23, option B and C look closely similar. But as Dave says, it's not the changing of options that is the problem but the availability of too many options. So the answer is B (the system cannot handle course options.)

Randhir: well, it sounds like you could do with an assistant but that's obviously not possible, so what about having an online system that **students can use to do their scheduling?**

> ➤ Again here, it might at first sound like Randhir is suggesting Dave should hire an assistant, which would make us select the option B. But he's asking Dave to put the system online for students to use it, making option A (students should create their own timetables) our correct answer.

Dave: how would that work?

Randhir: well- it may mean less choice for students but we could create a fixed schedule of all courses and options and they could then view what is available. But now we need to decide whether we need to replace the existing system or repair it.

Dave: well I'd prefer a new system. I've had enough of this one.

Randhir: okay, that'll probably take longer **although it may save you money in the long run.** When are you hoping to have this in place?

> ➤ Our correct answer for question 25 is option C (will be economical), because he clearly says that it will help them to save money, i.e. be more economical.

Dave: well **it's January now** and the new intake of students will be in September. We need to start processing admissions in next few weeks really.

Randhir: well, it will take more than few weeks, I'm afraid. As an initial estimate I think we'll be looking at **April or May** to improve the existing system but for a new system it would be at least nine months. That would be October.

> ➤ Please note that the questions asked about the time taken to improve the existing system and not about installing the new one, so the correct answer will be option B (four or five months), calculating from the time difference, instead of option C (nine months).

Keep In Mind

> ➤ The first thing you hear might not be the answer. Wait till the conversation about a single question gets over.

> ➤ Sometimes the speakers talk about all the options just to cancel them out. At that point, find out about the option that was not cancelled and mark it as your answer.

> ➤ Remember, there is no negative marking here, so if you miss the question then mark anything you think is close enough at the end of the section.

Hands-On

Try some of the examples yourself by reading the transcripts.

EXAMPLE 1

Choose the correct letter from A–D and mark your answers on your answer sheet.

1. According to the tutor, the basic criterion for evaluating the websites should relate to

   A. appearance.

   B. ease of use.

   C. target customers.

2. On the subject of timing, the tutor says

   A. the students' plan is appropriate.

   B. the students' presentation will be too long.

   C. the students can extend the presentation if necessary.

3. Sarah and Jack will share the work by

   A. speaking in short turns.

   B. doing half the presentation each.

   C. managing different aspects.

4. The tutor advises Sarah and Jack not to

   A. talk too much.

   B. show complicated lists.

   C. use a lot of visuals.

Tutor: OK, well you'd better stick to the most obvious differences, because you've only got ten minutes for the whole presentation, haven't you? And you said you're going to evaluate each site as well, didn't you? How are you going to do that? I mean what criteria will you use?

Sarah: We thought we'd use three criteria: how attractive each website is, how user-friendly, it is, and how closely it targets its potential customers. Do you think that's OK?

Tutor: Sounds fine. But I'd look at the criteria in a different order if I were you. Because really, you've got to look at attractiveness and user-friendliness in relation to the people the website is aiming at. So, I'd deal with that criterion first if I were you.

Sarah: Right.

Tutor: What about the timing? Have you thought of that? Ten minutes is very short you know.

Jack: Yes. We tried it out.

Sarah: Several times!

Jack: And we've decided to spend four minutes comparing the two sites, then three minutes evaluating them, and leave three minutes for questions. That's not really enough, but …

Tutor: Well it sounds about right to me. You've got ten minutes altogether and you have got to stick to that limit. It's good practice, and at least the audience won't have time to get bored! What visuals are you going to use?

Jack: We're going to use PowerPoint and a flip chart as well.

Sarah: So, we can show two things at once. For example, we're going to start by showing the Home Pages of each website, and we're going to put up a list of key features on the flip chart at the same time.

Tutor: OK. And it's a joint presentation, so have you decided how you're going to share the work?

Jack: Yes. First, we thought we'd keep taking it in turns to speak – Sarah would say a bit, then I'd take over, and so on. Then we thought we'd just divide it into two equal parts and do one part each. But it was all too complicated. So, Sarah's going to do all the talking, and I'm going to manage the visuals. And hope we can coordinate properly!

Sarah: It's the only way we can fit everything in.

Tutor: Well, good. You've obviously worked hard and you've been very careful with the details. Only one thing I would say: make sure that you keep your visuals simple. I mean, if you're showing a list of key features, for example, you should make it as brief as possible. Just use bullet points and simple phrases, even single words. Your audience won't have much reading time. It's a classic mistake with seminar presentations to present so much information that the audience can't process it quickly enough, and they stop listening to what you're saying. OK?

Jack: Yes. Right. OK.

Tutor: And now let's talk about…

Answers

1. C

2. A

3. C

4. B

EXAMPLE 2

Choose the correct letter from A-D and mark your answers on your answer sheet.

  1. These sessions with a counsellor are…

      A. compulsory for all students.

      B. available to any students.

      C. for science students only.

  2. The counsellor says that new students have to…

      A. spend more time on the college premises.

      B. get used to working independently.

      C. work harder than they did at school.

3. John complains that the resource centre…

   A. has limited opening hours.

   B. has too few resources.

   C. gets too crowded.

4. The counsellor suggests to John that…

   A. most other students can cope.

   B. he needs to study all the time.

   C. he should be able to fit in some leisure activities.

5. Before being able to help John the counsellor needs to…

   A. talk with some of his lecturers.

   B. consult his tutor.

   C. get more information from him.

Transcript

Counsellor: Hello, John, what can I do for you?

John: Well, I heard about these counselling sessions from a friend doing a science course and I was really interested. I think they should be compulsory, really.

Counsellor: Well, to be quite honest, John, I think they would be useful for everybody but, well, everybody has their own way of going about things. I prefer people just to drop in when they can.

John: Yes.

Counsellor: I find that talking to students about the requirements of a course helps to clarify what needs to be done. I mean the biggest difference between college and school is that new college students really have to do a lot of work on their own, and it's sometimes useful to get advice on how to take control of your time and work effectively.

John: Yes. I mean, it seems like a very light workload until assignment time comes and then I seem to be working all night sometimes. I'm not the only one. It's ridiculous. The resource centre is very good but it closes so early. It's in the library and so you'd think you could use it more. It's a real problem for me.

Counsellor: Well, you're certainly not the only person in that position, as I'm sure you've found. It really comes down to using every available hour in a systematic way. If you do this with a plan, then you'll find that you still have time for yourself and your hobbies as well.

John: Yeah. I've heard from Thomas that you made him a sort of plan like this, and he's going away for the weekend with all his work handed in, whereas I haven't even started.

Counsellor: I need to find out a few more things about you first. I'll give you this form to fill in about your lectures and things before you leave.

Counsellor: Now, what are your main problems?

John: Well, what most concerns me is I'm still not doing very well in my assignments.

Answers

1. B
2. B
3. A

4. C
5. C

EXAMPLE 3

Choose the correct letter from A-D and mark your answers on your answer sheet.

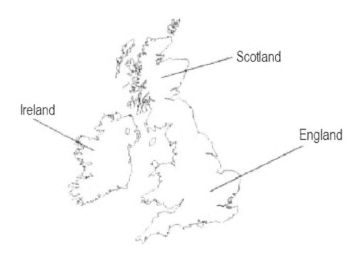

1. **According to the speaker, it is not clear**

   A. when the farming economy was introduced to Ireland.

   B. why people began to farm in Ireland.

   C. where the early Irish farmers came from.

2. **What point does the speaker make about breeding animals in Neolithic Ireland?**

   A. Their numbers must have been above a certain level.

   B. They were under threat from wild animals.

   C. Some species died out during this period.

3. **What does the speaker say about the transportation of animals?**

   A. Livestock would have limited the distance the farmers could sail.

   B. Neolithic boats were too primitive to have been used.

   C. Probably only a few breeding animals were imported.

4. **What is the main evidence for cereal crops in Neolithic Ireland?**

   A. the remains of burnt grain in pots.

   B. the marks left on pots by grains.

   C. the patterns painted on the surface of pots.

Transcript

Good morning everyone. Last week we were looking at the hunter-gatherers in Ireland, across the Irish Sea from England. Today, we're going to move on to the period between four and six thousand years ago, known as the Neolithic period, which is when a total farming economy was introduced in Ireland.

Now, there are several hypotheses about the origins of the first Neolithic settlers in Ireland, but most of these contain problems. For instance, there are considerable archaeological difficulties about the theory that they came from England. The evidence doesn't really add up. But there are even greater practical problems about the theory that they came directly from continental Europe. For one thing, it's not clear just how sufficient numbers of men and women could have been transported to Ireland to establish a viable population. As you know, the hunter-gatherer economy which existed beforehand was based on small scattered groups. The farming economy would almost certainly have required much larger communities to do all the work needed to plant and tend sufficient crops to sustain them through the year.

The early farmers kept various animals, including cattle and sheep. There's also evidence of pigs, but it is possible that these could have been descended from the native wild species.

Now, we know from modern farming that if the level of breeding stock falls below about three hundred females, the future of the species locally is at risk. So, we must assume that from the beginnings of Neolithic farming the number of breeding sheep would have considerably exceeded three hundred, and the national cattle herd must have been of a similar size. The question is how these were brought to the area and where they came from.

It's usually suggested that the Neolithic settlers used skin-covered boats to transport livestock. But this method would have severely restricted the range of the colonising fleets. The sheer volume of animal transport necessarily means it's unlikely that this livestock could have been brought from anywhere further than England.

What about crops? Well, two main cereal crops were introduced to Ireland during this time: wheat and barley, both in several varieties. The main evidence for their presence consists of impressions on pottery, where a cereal grain accidentally became embedded in the surface of a pot before it was fired. The grain itself was destroyed by the firing, but it left an impression on the pot which could be studied and identified by botanists

Answers

1. C

2. A

3. A

4. B

Maps

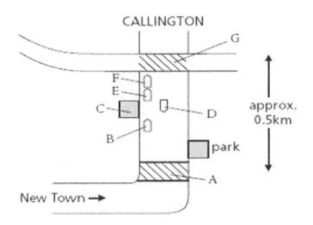

1. traffic lights _____

2. petrol station _____

3. blue van _____

Transcripts

Assistant 2: I don't know Callington at all, so could you describe it for me? Where did the accident happen?

Elisabeth: On the road between New Town and Callington. I was driving from New Town, heading towards Callington, and ...

Assistant 2: OK, just let me draw the road layout ... Right. OK?

Elisabeth: When you leave New Town there's a sharp bend in the road and then there's a railway bridge. (so, the marking A becomes railway bridge and that is not the answer)

Assistant 2: OK.

Elisabeth: And **then about half a kilometre further on there's a crossroads with traffic lights.** (look at the distance given in the map) And I was just in between the two when it happened. I wasn't going very fast, in fact I definitely …

Assistant 2: So, you'd already gone over the bridge?

Elisabeth: Yes. And I'd passed the park – that's on the right-hand side. And I was just approaching the petrol station …

Assistant 2: Where's that then?

Elisabeth: It's a bit further along, on the opposite side. (so, we mark petrol as C because it is the only stationary thing on the left)

Assistant 2: So, on your near side then?

Elisabeth: Yes. **As I was approaching it I saw a blue van coming towards me.** (it is the only van which is facing towards Elisabeth's car) The driver had stopped in the middle of the road.

Assistant 2: Was he indicating?

Elisabeth: Yes. He was waiting to turn into the petrol station. But then at the last minute, he decided to turn right in front of me. He must have thought he had enough time, but I had to swerve to avoid him. And I came off the road and landed in a ditch on the opposite side.

Assistant 2: Mmm. I don't suppose he stopped, did he?

Elisabeth: Oh yes. He came over to see if I was OK, but he tried to say it was my fault. And there wasn't

Answers

1. G

2. C

3. D

Keep In Mind

➤ Always look beforehand at where the map will start from. And look for the things around them. Is it going to be a street, a shop or a building? And listen to the recording accordingly.

➤ Look at the major parts of the map or plan to help you understand and navigate your way around.

➤ Although most of the times, the places are visited in sequential order, you still need to listen carefully to phrases like 'turn behind,' 'turn left,' 'crossover,' etc. Words like these will help you understand the map a bit better.

➤ Always follow the speaker's words with a finger and move where he tells you to go. This will ease your job.

Hands-On

Try some of the examples yourself by reading the transcripts.

EXAMPLE 1

Label the map below:

Write the correct letter, A–J next to questions 1–4

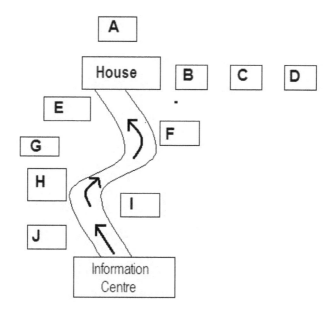

1. Pear Alley_____

2. Mulberry Garden_____

3. Shop_____

4. Tea Room_____

Transcript

Now, please look at the map I've given you of the house and gardens. We're here at the Information Centre. Follow the path marked with the arrow and the first area you come to is the orchard on your left.

As you go further down the path, there's the kitchen garden on the right and as you go round the first sharp corner you will find, to your left, an area where different types of pear tree have been planted as well as some lovely flowers, and this is known as Pear Alley-designed by George himself.

Next to this is the greenhouse where some exotic plants and fruits are grown. Follow the path round the second corner and on your right, you will see the entrance to the Mulberry Garden with its 500-year-old tree. Past the Mulberry Garden, follow the path until you reach the front of the house. I suggest you spend a good hour wandering around this lovely building. A guide takes visitor groups round every two hours.

If you would like to purchase any of George's books or other souvenirs, then leave the house by the side entrance, where you will find our shop, which is situated between the house and the garage which contains the magnificent old Rolls-Royce car which used to belong to George. I expect by this time you may also be in need of a rest and some refreshment. Most visitors are, so why don't you visit the tea room on the far side of the garage?

If you have time, there is a lovely walk down towards the River Dudwell. For me, this is the best part of the estate. This isn't on the map but it is all clearly signposted. You cross the field which spreads along the banks of the river. In spring, this area is well worth a visit.

Answers

1. H

2. F

3. B

4. D

EXAMPLE 2

Label the rooms on the map below.

Choose your answers from the box below and write them next to questions **1–5.**

CL	Computer Laboratory
DO	Director's Office
L	Library
MH	Main Hall
S	Storeroom
SAR	Self Access Room
SCR	Student Common Room
SR	Staff Room

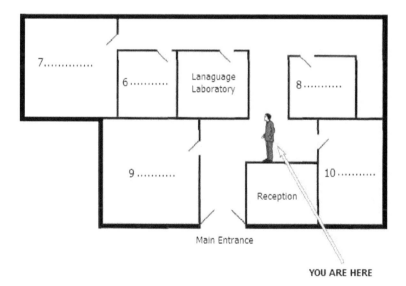

Transcript

Student: But how do I find the Main Hall?

Receptionist: Right; if you look on the back of the booklet I gave you, you'll see a map of the school. Let me show you. Look: you came in through the

Main Entrance, here, and now we're here at Reception. Now, to get to the Main Hall, you walk on to the end of this corridor in front of you and then you turn left. Walk along past the Language Laboratory and then past the Library, which is next to the Language Lab, on the same side, and facing you is the Main Hall, at the end of the corridor. You can't miss it.

Student: So, it's next to the Library, in fact.

Receptionist: Yes, that's right.

Student: I should be able to find that. And do you have a Computer Laboratory?

Receptionist: Yes, we do.

Student: Could you tell me where that is?

Receptionist: Certainly, yes. You go down to the end of this corridor again but, this time, don't turn left; turn right, away from the Main Hall. The Computer Lab. is immediately on your right. OK?

Student: And where's the staff room, in case I need to find a teacher at some stage?

Receptionist: The staff room is near the main entrance, on the left over there, just opposite the Reception desk. In a day or two, I'm sure you'll find your way around very easily.

Student: Oh, one last thing. Is there a student common room?

Receptionist: Oh yes, I forgot to mention that. It's this area here, very close to where we are now, to the right of the Reception desk as you come in the main entrance. There's tea and coffee facilities there.

Student: Great. Thank you very much.

Receptionist: You're welcome.

Answers

1. L

2. MH

3. CL

4. SR

5. SCR

WRITING TEST

FORMAT

➤ This writing module takes one hour to complete.

➤ The format and timing are same for both Academic and General modules.

➤ The entire module consists of two tasks: Task 1 and Task 2.

Training	General	Academic
Task 1 (150 words)	Letter	Report
Task 2 (250 words)	Essay	Essay

MARK SCHEME

The distribution of the masks is distributed as following:

➤ TASK 1 = 3 band

➤ TASK 2 = 6 band

DISTRIBUTION OF BAND

The respective markings of task 1 and task 2 are done on the following four pillars:

➤ Task achievement (task1) / task response (task2)

➤ Coherence and cohesion

➤ Lexical resource

➤ Grammatical range and accuracy

TIME DISTRIBUTION

You should not spend more than 20 minutes on task 1 and not more than 40 minutes on task 2.

> ➤ The rest of the instructions will be printed on the given question paper. Read it very carefully.

How to Handle Writing VOCABULARY

Since the lexical resources hold 25% of task 1, it becomes tricky to score full marks in this section. There is a wide range of vocabulary you might require in this section. For the same purpose, you might:

> ➤ Make use of correct synonyms in your writing.

> ➤ Use a wide range of words.

> ➤ Do not repeat words and phrases from the exam question unless there is no alternative.

> ➤ Use less common vocabulary words.

> ➤ Do not use the same word more than once/twice.

> ➤ Use precise and accurate words in a sentence.

TYPES OF TASK 1

1. Bar graph
2. Pie chart
3. Line graph
4. Table
5. Maps
6. Diagrams
7. Process

9 BAND CRITERIA

1. Task Achievement

i. Your task should fully satisfy all answers.

ii. Your response should be clearly represented.

2. Coherence and Cohesion

   i. You should use cohesion (binding the matter as a whole) in such a manner that it attracts no attention.

   ii. You need to manage the paragraphing skilfully.

   iii. Your data should not be misinterpreted.

   iv. Overall clarity of your report and message should be delivered.

3. Lexical Resources

   i. Use a wide variety of vocabulary with very natural and sophisticated control of lexical features.

   ii. Accurately and appropriately use the words/phrases given in the graph.

4. Grammatical Range and Accuracy

   i. Use a wide range of structures with full flexibility and accuracy.

   ii. Do not use the same style or phrase of comparison or explanatory sentences over and over again, as it causes repetition.

TASK 1

VOCABULARY

Look at the diagram below.

It will give you a brief idea of how to use various phrases for the different phases of a graph.

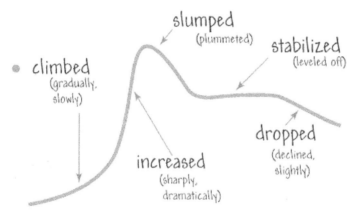

- Increase = rise / go up / uplift / rocketed / climb / upsurge / soar.

slumped
(plummeted)

stabilized
(leveled off)

climbed
(gradually,
slowly)

dropped
(declined,
slightly)

increased
(sharply,
dramatically)

- Cars = automobile, motor vehicle, vehicle.

INTRODUCTION PHRASES

Starting	Presentation Type	Verb	Description
The/the given/ the supplied/ the presented/ the shown/the provided	diagram/table/ figure/illustration/ graph/chart/flow chart/picture/ presentation/pie chart/bar graph/ column graph/line graph/table data/ data/information/ pictorial/ process diagram/ map/ pie chart and table/ bar graph and pie chart...	shows/represents/ depicts/enumerates/ illustrates/presents/ gives/provides/ delineates/ outlines/ describes/delineates/ expresses/ denotes/ compares/shows contrast/indicates/ figures/gives data on/gives information on/ presents information about/ shows data about/ demonstrates/sketch out/summarises...	the comparison of... the differences... the changes... the number of... information on... data on... the proportion of... the amount of... information on... data about... comparative data... the trend of... the percentages of... the ratio of... how the...

BREAKDOWN OF TASK 1

Introduction

Introduction with rephrasing of the topic (never rewrite the same lines) + Overview of general trend, i.e. what the diagrams indicate at a first glance.

Reporting Details

Main features in the details

   +Compare and contrast the data. (Do not give all the figures)

   +Most striking features of the graph.

Conclusion

Conclusion (General statement + Implications, significant comments)

[Conclusion is optional.]

VOCABULARY TO SHOW CHANGES

Trends	Verb Form	Noun Form
Increase	rise/increase/go up/uplift/ rocket(ed)/climb/upsurge/ soar/ shot up/ improve/ jump/ leap/ move upward/ skyrocket/ soar/ surge.	a rise/an increase/an upward trend/a growth/ a leap/a jump/an improvement/ a climb.
Decrease	fall/decrease/decline/ plummet/plunge/drop/ reduce/collapse/deteriorate/ dip/dive/go down/take a nosedive/slum/slide/go into free-fall.	a fall/a decrease/ a reduction/a downward trends/a downward tendency/a decline/ a drop/a slide/a collapse/ a downfall.
Steadiness	unchanged/level out/ remain constant/remain steady/plateau/remain the same/remain stable/remain static	a steadiness/a plateau/ a stability/ a static
Gradual Increase	_____	an upward trend/ an upward tendency/ a ceiling trend
Gradual Decrease	_____	a downward trend/ a downward tendency/ a descending trend
Standability Flat	level(ed) off/remain(ed) constant/remain(ed) unchanged/remain(ed) stable/prevail(ed) consistency/plateaued/ reach(ed) a plateau/stay(ed) uniform/immutable/ level(ed) out/ stabilise/ remain(ed) the same.	No change, a flat, a plateau

Type of Change	Adverb Form	Adjective Form
Rapid change	dramatically/rapidly/ sharply/quickly/hurriedly/ speedily/swiftly/significantly/ considerably/substantially/ noticeably.	dramatic/rapid/sharp/ quick/hurried/speedy/ swift/significant/ considerable/ substantial/noticeable.
Moderate Change	moderately/gradually/ progressively/sequentially.	moderate/gradual/ progressive/sequential.
Steady Change	moderate/gradual/ progressive/sequential.	Steady/ ceaseless
Slight Change	slightly/slowly/mildly/ tediously.	Slight/slow/mild/ tedious

PERCENTAGE, PORTION AND NUMBERS:

Percentages

10% increase, 25 percent decrease, increased by 15%, dropped by 10 per cent, fall at 50%, reached to 75%, tripled, doubled, one-fourth, three-quarters, half, double fold, treble, 5 times higher, 3 timers lower, declined to about 49%, stood exactly at 43%.

Fractions

4% = A tiny fraction.

24% = Almost a quarter.

25% = Exactly a quarter.

26% = Roughly one quarter.

32% = Nearly one-third, nearly a third.

49% = Around a half, just under a half.

50% = Exactly a half.

51% = Just over a half.

73% = Nearly three quarters.

77% = Approximately three quarter, more than three-quarter.

79% = Well over three quarters.

Proportions

2% = A tiny portion, a very small proportion.

4% = An insignificant minority, an insignificant proportion.

16% = A small minority, a small portion.

70% = A large proportion.

72% = A significant majority, A significant proportion.89% = A very large proportion.

89% = A very large proportion.

Writing Task 1

1. The bar graph below shows the computer ownership by education level in two years (2002 and 2010).

    Summarize the information by selecting and reporting the main features and make comparisons where relevant.

    Write at least 150 words.

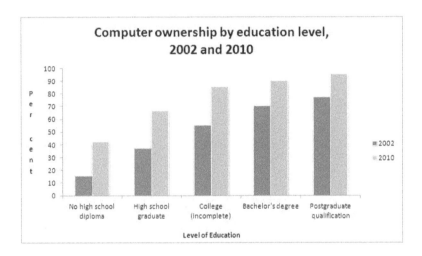

The bar graph above **enumerates/illustrates/presents** the number of computers owned by various education levels, in percentage. The data given is a **contrast** of two years over a duration of 8 years (2002–2010).

The first striking feature of the graph would be the percentage of higher secondary education exceeding 80% in all three college sectors in 2010. Conversely, the lower level of **education remains at a bracket of 40–65% of ownership.** For 2002, **the trends remained steady** with a different value in numbers. The higher levels of education held the ownership in the range of 55–75% approximately, whereas the lower levels struggled at around 15–35%.

Talking about the progress made in the span of 8 years, **it is clear that the** sector of no high school diploma makes an impressive mark with a progress of 30%, with an incomplete college career **being on par** with the number of people with degrees, along with high school graduates. The higher secondary levels remain in the numbers of an average 20% improvement.

Overall, **we can conclude that, although the** higher secondary levels still have a higher ownership of computers, it is the junior levels of education that show a tremendous amount of improvement and advancement.

2. **The pie chart gives information on UAE government spending in 2000. The total budget was AED 315 billion. It gives the information about where the money went.**

   Write a report describing the information given in the chart.

   Write in at least 150 words.

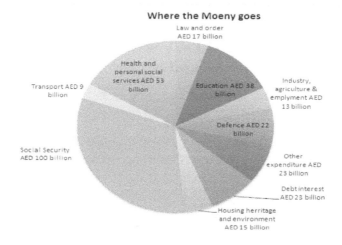

The **pie chart shows** the UAE government's budget spending in different sectors in 2000. The pie chart **illustrates the expenditure** of the UAE government from the national budget 315 billion AED in 2000. It also **represents the segments** of expenditure of the UAE administration in different sectors in the same year.

It is crystal clear from the pie chart that the UAE administration allocated AED 100 billion in social security from their national budget of AED 315 billion. This single sector cost the UAE government

almost one-third of the total budget. This year the government's expense was 53 million on health and personal social services, which **was the second largest sector** in terms of expenditure. AED 38 million was spent on education, while 23 billion both in debt and other expenditures.

Moving further, **it is vivid that** the government used 22 billion in the Defence sector, while 13 billion went towards the industry, employment and agriculture sectors. **The lowest amount of money,** only 9 billion, went to the transport sector. Finally, 15 billion of the budget was spent on housing and environment.

Overall, **it can be deduced** that the UAE government's maximum spending went in the social security and healthcare sectors, while the least amounts were spent on transport, law and order, housing and industry/agriculture and employment sectors.

3. **The graph below shows radio and television audiences throughout the day in 1992.**

   Summarize the information given by reporting and selecting the main features and make comparisons wherever necessary.

   Write in at least 150 words.

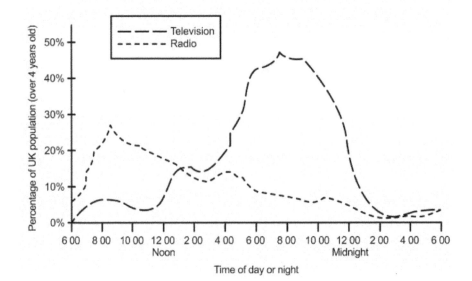

Radio and television audiences in UK, October – December 1992

The line graph **gives us information regarding** the spectators of both radio and television throughout the day in December of 1992 in the United Kingdom.

The first striking feature of the graph is that, when the day starts, around 10% of people tune into the radio. Right at 6 o'clock in the morning, the people turn on the radio. **And the radio enjoys this popularity** until2 in the afternoon. **The peak hour of** radio is at around 8 in the morning, where nearly **one-third of people** listen to the radio. And as the day goes by, the audience of radio decreases, falling to an average of mere 5–6%.

Contrasting the viewed hours of television, it is not very fondly watched in the morning. But as the day continues, the people watching television **also increases manifold.** Right from noon, the watchers start to tune into their respective T. V sets, and all the way till 2 am it **enjoys a drastic amount of viewership.** The peak timing is 8 o'clock in the evening, **where around 50% of people tune in.**

In the end, **we can conclude that** as the day goes on, the popularity of the radio decreases as the popularity of television grows stronger. Radio is only the favourite among masses in the morning.

4. **The given diagram shows the difference between a city named Denham.**

Write a report telling main features and make comparisons where necessary.

Write in at least 150 words.

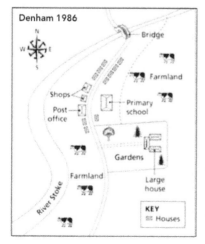

The **two given pictorials** depict the **contrast of the city** of Denham over a span of 30 years, from 1986 to 2016.

At first glance, we can notice that there many things in the city which have changed and there are still many which are pretty much the same. **The first thing we notice is** that, in the name of development, there has been a construction of a plethora of houses on the areas where there used to be farmlands and gardens. The primary school has been further developed, and the large **house has been converted** into a retirement home. The post office near the shop **has vanished in 30 years, whereas** the shops next to it remain intact.

We can also see that there has **been an introduction of some** new roads as well so that they can be used to facilitate the housing more conveniently. **Another unchanged feature** in the two pictures is that the river and the bridge over the river **remain untouched and unchanged.**

5. **The given table shows the population of different animals according to the year.**

   Summarize the information and make comparisons where necessary.

   Write in at least 150 words.

TIME	POPULATION				
	Elephant	Giraffe	Ostrich	Zebra	Rhino
1977	1496	4745	239	37403	216
1980	1281	3703	224	27372	0
1983	1413	3094	195	45000	0
1986	1229	2235	480	21823	14
1990	1151	1559	420	25216	0

The table **shown above outlines the population** of 5 types of animals over a time span of 13 years given in 5 different years.

The most satisfying and striking numbers are held by the animal zebra with its numbers ranging from 45,000+ to 25,000+. **Zebra hit the lowest number** in year 1986 and recovered itself in next 4 years.

The second position held in the terms of numbers is by giraffe with its population not exceeding 5000 and not declining below 1500. Next turn is held up by elephants with **its numbers being stable** around 1200 approximately.

On the other hand, ostrich is the only animal in the **lot who has multiplied and increased its number** almost to the **double level.**

The most saddening and unfortunate numbers are showcased in the scenario of rhino, which **over just a time lapse of 3 years got extinct.** Even the 14 rhinos found in year 1986 could not help and again vanished in next three years up to 1990.

6. **The given image shows the process of recycling the glass bottles through various stages and steps.**

   Summarize the information in at least 150 words.

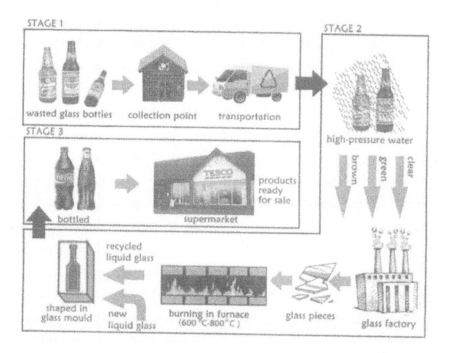

The **pictorial above is a diagram** explaining the process of recycling glass bottles and how to reuse them in a new form. The **process includes various** steps, and 3 stages in all.

Stage 1 **clearly depicts** the simple steps of collecting old glass bottles at a single collection point. After collecting these bottles, they are sent somewhere else through the transportation facility. **In the next** stage, the transferred bottles are washed under high-pressure water. and all the three types of bottles—namely green, brown and clear—are sent to the glass factory, where they are broken into the glass pieces. These glass pieces are burnt in a furnace at a temperature ranging from 600–800 degrees Celsius. **The combination of this** old recycled liquid glass and some new liquid glass is then added in glass moulds to get the desired shape.

After finishing stage 2, we enter the next stage, where these glass bottles are used to bottle beverages and sent to the supermarket, where the products are ready for sale.

7. **The flowchart below gives information about the drawbacks of the clear cutting of forests.**

   Summarize the points given in at least 150 words.

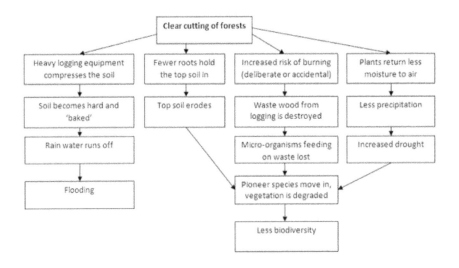

The presentation above expresses the concerns regarding the clear cutting of forests through a flow chart, **providing information on** why it is a hazard to the environment. The chart is divided into 4 main parts.

The first series of flow shows us the drawbacks deforestation has on the soil. It says that heavy logging compresses the soil, which makes the soil baked and gives way to water to run down and cause floods.

The next flow warns about the reduced number of roots inside the soil, which results in top soil erosion and degradation in vegetation.

Clear cutting of forests also increases the risk of burning forests, which maybe accidental or deliberate, **leading to a wastage of logs** that get destroyed due to burning. Micro-organisms then feed on the wasted lot, and pioneer vegetation species get destroyed, which results in less biodiversity overall.

It further explains the hazardous consequences of clearing forests, narrating that plants return less moisture to the air, which in turn reduces precipitation and increases the droughts.

Conclusively, **it is crystal clear** that clearing up forests has no positive effect on the natural environment.

Hands-On

QUESTION 1: The charts below show the results of a survey about what people of different age groups say makes them most happy.

Summarise the information by selecting and reporting the main features and make comparisons where relevant.

Write at least 150 words.

What makes people most happy?

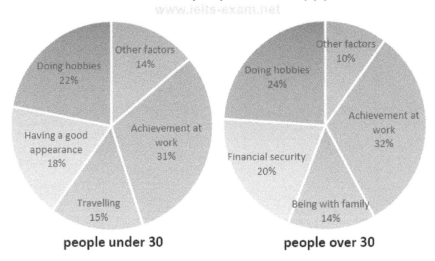

people under 30   people over 30

QUESTION 2: The table below shows the number of students living in the UK gaining English language teacher training qualifications in 2007/8 and 2008/9, and the proportion of male qualifiers.

Summarise the information by selecting and reporting the main features and make comparisons where relevant.

Write at least 150 words.

Qualifications for English Language Teachers obtained 2007/8 and 2008/9, UK		Total	Female	Male	% Male
2007/8	Total	32,930	23,842	8,165	24.7%
	TEFL	25,446	18,460	6,870	26.9%
	Cambridge UCLES CELTA & other degrees	7,484	5,382	1,295	17.3%
2008/9	Total	32,945	24,324	7,511	22.7%
	TEFL	24,917	18,446	6,545	26.2%
	Cambridge UCLES CELTA & other degrees	8,028	5,878	966	12.1%

QUESTION 3: The diagrams below show the changes that have taken place at Queen Mary Hospital since its construction in 1960.

Summarise the information by selecting and reporting the main features and make comparisons where relevant.

Write at least 150 words.

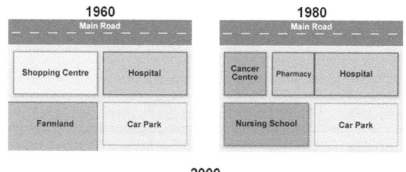

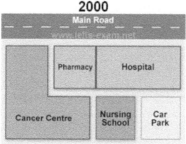

QUESTION 4: The graph below shows the number of books read by men and women at Burnaby Public Library from 2011 to 2014.

Summarise the information by selecting and reporting the main features and make comparisons where relevant.

Write at least 150 words.

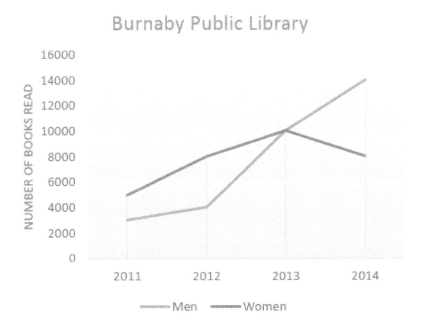

QUESTION 5. The charts give information about two genres of TV programmes watched by men and women and four different age groups in Australia.

Summarise the information by selecting and reporting the main features and make comparisons where relevant.

Write at least 150 words.

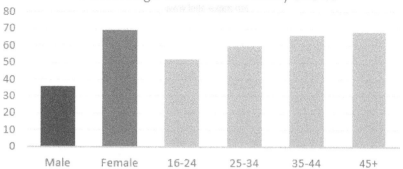

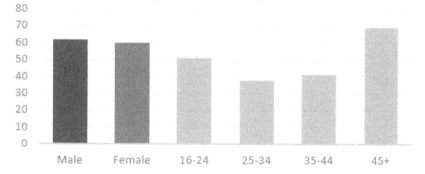

GENERAL
TRAINING

Solved Examples of Informal Letter

You want to sell your television. You think a friend of yours might like to buy it from you. Write a letter to your friend.

In your letter:

➢ Explain why you are selling the television.

➢ Describe the television.

➢ Suggest a date when your friend can come and see it.

Write at least 150 words

You do NOT need to write any addresses

Begin your letter as follows:

Dear.........,

Model Answer

Dear Gary,

Hope you are doing well.

I'm doing fine, though my life is quite hectic at the moment because, as you know, I am moving abroad and there is so much to do.

There are a few things that I can't take with me because they are not portable. So I am seeing if any of my friends would be interested in buying them. One of the things I do not wish to take with me is my television, and I thought you might be interested in purchasing it from me at a cheaper price.

It's a 32″ flat screen TV, and it's a Phillips model. It has a USB port, so you can just plug in a thumb drive to watch movies or listen to music. It has great stereo surround sound quality.

As you know, I am flying by the end of this month, which is only two weeks away. So if you are keen to buy my television kindly update me with the same as soon as you can. Perhaps otherwise, I look for another buyer.

Kindly revert back to me and let me know as soon as you can.

All the best,

John

Unsolved Examples of Personal: Informal Letter

1. You play a team sport with some friends. Last week, a member of the team had an accident and wasn't able to play with you over the weekend. You decide to write to him in hospital, telling him about the match.

    Write a letter to your friend. In your letter,

    - Tell him which team won.
    - Describe the conditions on the day.
    - Say how you felt about the match.

2. You have a friend who lives in a different country. You will organize a party soon and have thought to use a foreign recipe. Write a letter to the friend asking for a recipe from his/her country for the party you are organizing.

    - Tell your friend about the party.
    - Ask for the recipe.
    - Explain why you need the recipe from his/her country.

Solved Examples of Semiformal Letter

You are experiencing financial problems and want to ask your landlord if you can pay your rent late. Write a letter to your landlord.

In your letter, explain:

➢ Why you are writing to him

➢ Why you cannot pay the rent

➢ When you will pay the rent.

Write at least 150 words

You do NOT need to write any addresses

Begin your letter as follows:

Dear.........,

Model Answer

Dear Mr. Strickland,

I am writing this letter to request you to allow me to pay the rent late.

I've been a tenant with you for a number of years now, and, as you know, I have always been sincere in paying my rent on time. However, unfortunately I am having a few financial problems at the moment. Last month, I switched my job to another firm and I am currently on a probation period for one month. My pay check is delayed because of the new job that I have started and as my company doesn't pay until 3 weeks have passed.

I would be highly obliged if you allow me to pay the rent by the 15th of next month. I assure and promise you that I would certainly not ask for the extension again. Once I get my first check, I will be able to pay the rent, as agreed in our lease.

I hope you will agree to the 15 days delay. Please contact me as soon as possible at […insert your phone no…]. In case, it is not suitable to you, we can surely discuss other options.

Yours sincerely,

John Streetham

Unsolved Examples of Semi Formal Letter

1. You are looking for a part-time job at a football club.

    Write a letter to the manager of the football club. In your letter,

    - Introduce yourself.

    - Explain what experience and special skills you have.

    - Tell him/her when you think you could start.

2. You saw an advertisement for a tennis course in England but you have one or two problems and can't stay the whole course.

    Write a letter to the course director. In your letter,

    - Explain your interest in the course.

    - Describe the problems.

    - Find out if a refund is possible.

Solved Examples of Formal Letter

Your car insurance company has told you that they are going to increase the amount you have to pay in insurance for your car each month. You are not happy about this.

Write a letter to your insurance company. In your letter explain

➤ Why you are writing to them

➤ Why you think the insurance should not be increased

➤ What you want them to do

Write at least 150 words

Dear Sir/Madam,

I am writing to you as I recently received a letter from you informing me that the insurance premium for my car is going to increase from next month.

If you verify my previous records, you will come to know that I have been a credible customer with your insurance company for nearly seven years now. During this time, I have never had an accident and never had any reason to make a claim on my insurance.

I understand that, according to new policies of your company, there is a hike in the prices. However, this increase you are suggesting will result in a 20% increase in the amount I pay each month, which is a rate I feel is too unreasonable.

I would therefore, be grateful if you could explain me the reasons behind such an increase that has been proposed from your end. In case of an unsatisfactory explanation, I will be left with no other recourse but to move my insurance to another company.

Kindly look into the matter and do the needful.

Yours faithfully,

Mr. Mahmoud Khan

Unsolved Examples of Formal Letter

1. The road in front of your house got damaged a long ago and nothing has been done about it. Write a letter to the municipal authority complaining about the damaged road.

   - Introduce yourself

   - Explain the condition of the road

   - Suggest what they should do

2. You are looking for a part-time job. Write a letter to an employment agency.

   - Introduce yourself.

   - Explain what sort of job you would like.

   - Say what experience and skills you have.

TASK 2

Tips and Types

TIPS

➢ **Understand:** Try to note down or think about what the question wants you to do. If possible try to make a brief outline or spider chart of the topic so that you know beforehand what you are going to write about.

➢ **Identify:** Note the type of question. Find out the trend and then add examples and relevant situations to make it more impactful.

➢ **Start:** Then start writing your task 2 with the suitable start.

TYPES:

1. **Opinion Essay Questions:** These types of questions ask about your opinion on a single topic and ask to what level or extent you agree or disagree.

   Example: Scientists and technology experts seem to be more valued by modern society than musicians and artists.

   To what extent do you agree or disagree?

2. **Discussion Type Questions:** These are questions that ask your opinion on both sides and ask you to discuss it.

   Example: Some people think that exercise is the key to health, while others feel that having a balanced diet is more important.

   Discuss both sides and give your opinion.

3. **Solution Essay Questions:** When this type of essay is asked, then you need to support your answer by giving reasons and solutions for a specific problem.

   Example: Overpopulation in urban centres around the world is a major problem. What are the causes of it? How can it be solved?

4. **Direct Question Essay Title:** This essay type can also be called two-question essays. It might also have more than two questions and will ask you to answer all of them with suitable explanations and examples.

   Example: Most people agree that money cannot buy happiness. Why is happiness difficult to define? How can we achieve happiness?

5. **Advantage/Disadvantage Questions:** As the name suggests, these essay types ask you to write some advantages and some disadvantages of a topic.

   Example: Space explorations cost taxpayers an exorbitant amount of money each year. What are the advantages and disadvantages of this trend?

Common Problems

1. **Talking too generally about the topic.**

   Most of these essays start off with 'Nowadays...' or 'In modern life...' followed by general information about the topic. Remember to be specific about the topic that has been asked and not beat around the bush.

2. **Outlining what you are going to do**

   If you don't include a sentence outlining what your essay will say, the examiner doesn't really know what you are going to write about in the rest of your essay. This will eventually affect your score. I'll show you how to write an outline sentence below.

3. **Using good vocabulary**

   What is advised to the students is to be always precise and stick to the topic. In order to have an extraordinary piece of writing, always keep in mind to use the vocabulary words.

4. **Using formal style**

   Know your audience. You are expected to write in an academic style.

Structure of a Good Introduction

If you use this structure, you will not only score higher bands but you will also save time in the exam. If you practice enough, you will be able to write introductions in very little time. This will provide you with sufficient time to emphasise on the main body paragraphs, which will help you get a good score.

IELTS writing task 2 opinion essay should have three sentences, and these three sentences should be:

1. Paraphrase question

2. Thesis statement

3. Outline statement

Let's look at each sentence in more detail.

1. Paraphrase Question

Paraphrasing means, stating the question again but with different words that have the same meaning. We do this by using synonyms and flipping the order of sentences around.

2. Thesis Statement

This is the central idea of your essay that gives direction to developing the body paragraphs 1 and 2. It tells the examiner that you have understood the question and will lead to a clear and coherent essay.

3. Outline Statement

Now that you have paraphrased the question and told the examiner what you think in your thesis statement, you are going to tell the examiner what you will discuss in the main body paragraphs. In other words, you will outline what the examiner will read in the rest of the essay.

1. **Advertisements are the most important marketing strategy to enhance the sale of products? Do you agree or disagree?**

Advertising is a mode used to multiply the sales of a product. Different modes and mediums are used to convey the message among the masses. An advertisement is of two types: electronic and print. Both are very important, but electronic is very popular and effective because it has a very strong audio-visual impact, and even role models are used to convey the message.

Iagree with the statement that advertising is an important marketing strategy, because the main motive is to create desire, which leads to demand and generates enough supply to give profits to the organization. No doubt, the burden of advertisements is shifted to the consumers, but the company makes a brand and enjoys the profit.

Expanding the statement, advertisements are becoming a mandatory part of sales. Earlier, people were happy with the local brands, whereas nowadays the market is flooded with internationally branded products. The competition is on global level and it is very tough to compete in the market, so it is not practically possible to survive in the business world without advertisement.

To recapitulate, advertising is a big industry that deals with the promotion of products. Social media has created a complete revolution in making choices for the consumer. But apart from it being a great market strategy, it is equally important to keep a check on the misleading advertisements in order to protect the interests of the consumers. The advertisements should not exaggerate the capability of the product or the performance of the product.

Vocabulary Words:

1. Adverts – advertisements
2. Product placement – how to put ads in movies
3. Celebrity endorsements – ads by celebrities
4. Word of mouth – publicity done by people themselves
5. Brand loyalty – blind trust on one brand
6. Mass media
7. Target audience
8. Viral – rapid circulation

2. **Tourism generates revenue, therefore it should be promoted. Discuss the statement and give solutions for its promotion.**

Tourism is the biggest industry of any country. There can be national or international tourists. Both types contribute towards the progress of the country. There are different types of tourism, like social, historical, religious and medical., Nowadays, due to effective means of transportation and communication, tourism industry is at its peak.

I agree with the statement that tourism industry is a very big contributor in regulating the country socially, economically and politically. It develops international relations and encourages cultural fusion. Moreover, it gives a boost to the economy by generating jobs and increasing per capita income. Similarly, political relations become strong, and tourists feel free enough to migrate. Analysing further, the tourist industry is very difficult to ignore. Government should come up with suitable laws to promote this industry.

To recapitulate, tourism is the biggest industry of any country. To promote tourism is a major objective of many politicians and bureaucrats at national and local levels. To understand what levers to attract new visitors is their greatest challenge. Choosing a place to visit is a voluntary act by an individual traveller who faces with incredible variety of offers, and then eventually chooses one that nearly meets his budget and makes him feel that it can guarantee the well-being that he seeks. Offering unique promotions such as tour discounts, online promo codes, gift cards and vouchers all can be used to attract the tourists and motivate them to book immediately.

Vocabulary Words:

1. Destination
2. Journey
3. Passengers
4. Cruise – to randomly roam in an area
5. Excursion
6. Budget
7. Infrastructure – buildings in an area
8. Local communities

3. **Millions of people every year move to English-speaking countries in order to get a better education. Why do many people want to learn English? Should they learn English in their own country and migrate or should they learn both the languages? Support your answer with reasons.**

Communication is a two-step process of interchanging ideas in a group or with an individual. English is an international language that has a very strong binding factor globally. It helps in developing international relations and provides global vision in the society.

In my opinion, language should be learnt from the native country, because translation is the only mode and medium to understand the concepts. Moreover, a student can study and work simultaneously, so it becomes very easy to adjust to a foreign culture. As suchit is advisable to have a beforehand understanding of the language.

Expanding the statement, the demand for English language has increased over the period, because in most of the jobs, good command over English language is a prerequisite. In the past, most of the students migrated for doing manual jobs. However, nowadays, awareness is high and students desire to polish their skills and work for white-collar jobs that are possible only with an understanding of a language. The student even feels comfortable with their regular studies in when the language is understandable.

To recapitulate, English-speaking countries are developed nations where students migrate for a better career, therefore non English-speaking countries should improve the quality of language at the primary level so that the students face less difficulties with the language when they migrate

Vocabulary Words:

1. Dialogue

2. Speech

3. Monologues – a speech by one person

4. Discussion

5. Language

6. Debate – discussion on two opposite topics

7. Non-verbal communication

8. Polyglot – a person who can speak more than two languages

4. **Communicating with other people in person, face to face is better than communicating with them by telephone or email. Do you agree or disagree?**

Communication is a two-way process for interchanging of ideas and views. Different modes and mediums are used to convey the message and develop relationships. The common medium is face to face which is personal and interactive. On the other hand, cell phones and emails are a complete revolution in the communication process.

Digital communication like cell phones and emails are trending because of the hectic and busy lifestyle. Practically it is not possible to meet every day. Moreover, to combat the distance and to maintain the relations cell phones, Face Time, Skype or email are solutions.

Expanding the statements further, face to face communication establishes more trust than other modes of communication. It is more likely to be perceived as credible. Face to face communication allows for better rapport and trust building than audio or written communication. It is more efficient and there is less likelihood for misunderstanding or misinterpretation.

To recapitulate, undoubtedly technological advancement have made the world easy to communicate. With a busy life and other easy way of communication people are avoiding face to face communication, but then undisputedly nothing can replace the value of face to face communication. It is only through face to face communication we can establish personal relations. Furthermore, face to face communication can eliminate isolation and stress that can come from sitting alone and by merely depending upon technology.

5. **Learning a new language at an early age is helpful for children. Is it more important for their future aspect or have some adverse effects? Do you agree or disagree?**

Children are the future of country, and this is the most tender section of society. They are immature, inexperienced and absolutely helpless. So, to engineer their plans in the right direction, a channel is required. As language is the base of education and communication, a child learns national, international and regional languages. Due to the impact of globalization, learning different languages is becoming part and parcel of daily necessity.

Learning new languages as a child, provides with lifetime benefits from cross-cultural friendships, broader career opportunities, exciting travel adventures and deeper insights into how others see the world. Learning new language also increases opportunities for connection and opens the door to many benefits of bilingualism. Studies have shown that people who are bilingual are better at work, that requires multi-tasking and attention focusing rather than children who are monolinguals. Further explaining, in fact, some researchers argue that the best way to have smarter kids is to expose them to multiple languages when they are young.

Years ago people believed that learning a second language would confuse a child. Now, research shows that children who study new languages perform better in their native language than non-bilingual students, as measured on standardized tests.

Why Children Learn Fast

- Children have keen interest in learning a new language.
- They are open-minded.
- They are full of energy and enthusiasm.
- They have high receptive skills, which makes them inquisitive for better performance.
- They understand very quickly and do not hesitate to practice the language.
- It's a young age, where in hesitation is low.

Benefits of Teaching Languages

- It prepares them for better future planning and helps develop to international relations.
- Multinational companies always encourage multilingual skills.
- As children are flexible and always inquisitive, so they learn fast.
- Receptivity is higher.

To recapitulate learning different languages is highly beneficial at the primary stage. It is a stage which is critical period for language acquisition, when the brain of a child is primed to learn. On the other hand at the later age, the aptitude for second language acquisition is reduced. Thus the advantages of learning new language at an early age is manifold. Many jobs in education, healthcare, social work, national security, tourism and international business require or favour candidates who are bilingual, resulting in more job opportunities for those who can speak a second language. Perhaps to boost the career opportunities and for a better future of the child it is essential that importance of learning new languages at his early stage of life is kept in mind.

Vocabulary Words:

1. Intensive course – two courses studying together

2. Diploma

3. Online/distant education

4. Vocational course – specialist course

5. Enrolment – take admission

6. Hypothesis

7. Tutorials/tutors

8. Assignment

9. Bilingual – speaking two languages fluently

---

6. **Artists and scientists play equally important roles. According to your opinion, who should be given more importance?**

An artist is a person who paints the world with his creative skills. He is highly imaginative and puts his best foot forward to carve out his skills in the best way possible. Imagination can be in the form of stage performance, story writing, painting or any other show, whereas a scientist is a person who with logical application of mind, tries to give concrete shape to the imagination of an artist. A scientist works for the comfort of the human race and can take ideas from the artist.

Role of Scientists:

- Both should be given equal importance. – Both possess the quality of perseverance. They spend countless hours on their craft and have to persevere through the failed attempts, till they are able to achieve the desired results.

- They promote industries, machines and modern techniques to further benefit society.

- People require advanced hospitals and medicines for better living conditions.

- They work on understanding and combating various diseases or create new technologies to meet the needs of the society.

Role of Artists:

- An artist is a great performer but does not deal with research or discovery.

- They give peace of mind to the people.

- They have more value in developed countries, where the people have basic amenities of already leading a comfortable life.

- They have the capacity to spend money on pieces of art.,

According to me, both should be given equal importance. The government should spend money on the promotion of the latest techniques for scientists. And it should give the artists the opportunity to portray and depict their talents on the stage in front of the public.

Vocabulary Words:

1. Creative
2. Classical
3. Musical/opera/theatre
4. Exhibition/sculpture/abstract – types of art
5. Genome/genetic – related to hereditary and genes of a person
6. Cyber – related to computers and online system
7. Marvels – wonders
8. Engineering/cloning

7. **Does modern technology make life more convenient or was life better when technology was simpler?**

Science is a logical application with different experiments, which lead to research, discovery and innovations. This technology makes life very fast, comfortable and well-organised. It also increases working efficiency and makes work effortless. Nowadays, science and technology forms a life force that contributes to regulate our daily lives.

Analysing the statement, it is quite evident that science and technology have made the world a better place to live, because they make overall progress socially, economically and politically. From accessing massive amounts of information on the internet to simply experiencing an enriched personal lifestyle, technology continues to benefit us regularly. It is true that technology is an important part of our daily lives.

Nowadays, most people have computers, laptops, tablets and even smartphones. These devices have made communication easier. Now we can browse the internet from anywhere, anytime. These devices have made life more enjoyable. No doubt earlier when technology was not advanced life was simpler but with the advent of technology and keeping in mind the present pace with which our lives are moving the dependence on technology is unavoidable. For instance, earlier communication used to be a lot of hassle. To communicate, people use to write letters. The recipient had to wait for days and even months. Nowadays, people normally use text messages and emails to pass important messages to colleagues and relatives.. Another, major contribution with the advent of technology is that travel industry has seen a huge change. Nowadays, we can easily locate places by using Google earth maps and so on. By just installing an app in our smartphones we can locate places. This is extremely helpful especially when we are travelling. In addition, to this it also helps us to locate our next destination conveniently.

To recapitulate, technology has without any doubt, contributed in spreading knowledge around the world, allowing for better advances in many fields. The increased spread of knowledge and ease of communication has allowed second and third world countries to advance more quickly. Hence to conclude modern technology and its inventions thereto, has helped in accomplishing many things in much easier manner than before.

Vocabulary Words:

1. Indispensable – something without which work cannot be done

2. Innovative – something creative and different

3. Device

4. E-commerce – online business

5. Modify – change to make better

6. Breakthrough – new discovery

7. Obsolete – not used anymore

8. Cutting-edge – smart/new technology

---

8. Parents should legally be held responsible for their children's acts. What is your opinion?

Family is a group of kith and kin living together and supporting each other. It is the first school from where one learns moral and ethical values. Undisputedly, children learn from their surroundings and, concurrent to this, their upbringing also plays a vital role to define their conduct and behavioural patterns in the society. But the fact cannot be ignored that it is a moral binding of the parents to nurture the child and make him/her a good citizen for society.

Analysing the statement, it is practically unfair to punish the parents for the criminal act of the child. It's the transitional age where there are biological and mental changes. Unless the parents have aided in helping the child to commit the crime they should never be held responsible for the child's action. Unfortunately, mentality of our society is such that if a child commits a crime it's always the parents that are blamed and the way a child is brought up is always questioned.

Expanding the statement and correspondingly analysing it further, it is unfair to support the ideology that parents should be punished, because parents already undergo deep pain with the antisocial behaviour of the child, as the bond between the two is pure, with unconditional love and high hopes.

To recapitulate, for the best upbringing of the child there should be a high level of counselling, orientations and awareness programmes, in which they learn to correct the behaviour of the child, which would help to reduce juvenile crime.

Vocabulary Words:

1. Nuclear family

2. Extended family – family including your uncles and aunts

3. Single-parent

4. Adolescents – age period before teenage and after childhood

5. Dependents

6. Guardian – elders acting as parents

7. Dysfunctional family – family which has some disputes amongst themselves

8. Foster – adopted family

---

9. **In underdeveloped countries, tourism has disadvantages. The opposite can be said as well.**

Positives of Tourism:

Social, Economic and Political

   i. **Personal Perspective:** Tourism is a popular leisure activity. Tourists can relax, have fun, 'recharge their batteries' and experience different cultures (sightseeing, sunbathing, visiting monuments, tasting new cuisines). Travelling opens our minds. It can broaden our horizon.

   ii. **Economic Perspective:** The tourism industry is vital for some countries. People rely on tourism for their income. Tourism attracts investment from governments and companies. It creates employment due to the demand for goods and services (hotels, entertainment, etc.).

Negatives of Tourism:

   i. **Environmental perspective:** Unsustainable practices by the tourism industry can thus lead to deforestation, sand erosion, loss of species, changes in sea currents and coastlines, destruction of habitats etc. Even activities like nature walks can be harmful to the environment if tourists trample on the local vegetation during their walk.

ii. **Socio-Cultural influences:** Local traditions may be lost. Tourists often, out of ignorance or carelessness, fail to respect local customs and moral values. When they do, it can lead to irritation among the local population.

iii. **Increase in crime rate:** Many people believe that tourism is the reason for the increase of illegal behaviour and higher rates of criminality. The results of this study estimates the involvement of tourists in various kinds of criminal activities.

To recapitulate, I hold my perception that global tourism brings benefits to the economic conditions of the country, enhancing the living standard of the person and letting them experience cross-country culture and customs. However, there are some detrimental effects which can be minimized by proper planning and governance. According to my opinion, a country should seek to develop its tourism industry, because it can bring steady jobs to many people and also can help in improving the GDP of the country.

10. **Stress is increasing rapidly among all the age groups. Discuss the reasons and give its solutions.**

Stress is an undue pressure on the mind that makes a person highly disturbed. It can almost happen at every age group and differs from person to person. Stress is always created by unachievable goals and ambitions. Stress is generally related with the outer circumstances and experiences of a person.

There are many reasons for stress.

i. When a person is unable to achieve his goals, he becomes stressful.

ii. Stress can be personal or professional.

iii. Social pressures can be big reasons for a stressful life.

iv. High level of competition is causing stress in the society.

v. People nowadays do not believe in simple living.

vi. Fall of culture and traditions is uprooting the society.

Solutions:

Social support should be adopted, such as seeking advice, counselling and motivation from experienced persons..

A person should be organised and target achievable goals.

Logical thinking should be encouraged to reduce stress. A timetable should be made to utilize hobbies, meditate, attend workshops and play.

Exercising is one of the most important methods that one can include in his daily routine to reduce stress. As it is proved and even advised by doctors that keeping our body and mind healthy and fit, helps to reduce anxiety and stress.

Another way to take control on your stress is to prioritise what needs to be done and make time for it.

Vocabulary Words:

1. Anxiety – feeling of worry or nervousness

2. Panic/crisis – time of difficulty

3. Muddled thinking – when you are not able to think clearly

4. Impaired judgement – making silly decisions

5. Depression

6. Apathy – feeling of pity and sorrow for someone else

7. Alienation – feeling of isolation and alone

8. Restlessness – inability to relax

---

11. **Worker often have to retire at the age of 60 or 65. However, some people say that they should be allowed to continue working for as long as they want.**

What is your opinion about this?

It is a common practice, in most of societies worldwide, for people to stop working when they reach the sixth decade of their life. This is because it has been observed that, with the passage of time, an individual's ability to perform goes downhill and thus has to be replaced by the youthful ideas.

One important reason why I believe that a person should call it a day at this age, is to give chance to the younger task force. The younger people have modern ideas and knowledge about the latest technology, but they can only put their ideas into practice when they get the opportunity to work. This is possible only when the older people retire and younger ones take their place. In addition, if the seniors continue to work, unemployment results. For instance, research carried out by the employment department revealed that many vacancies could be created if it is made mandatory for people to retire at the age of 60 or 65.

Not only that, but there are also other arguments that support retirement at a certain age. The reflexes get affected due to health issues that one faces with age, which affects their productivity. For example, greying workers take more sick leaves as compared to their younger counterparts. Hence, this also brings home the idea of compulsory retirement at a certain age.

In conclusion, I would like to reiterate that a person should cease to work at a particular age as it is good for him as well as for society. Society gets infused with new ideas, and the individual also gets the much-needed rest after having worked for the better part of his life.

12. **Some people believe that teaching children at home is best for a child's development while others think that it is important for children to go to school.**

    Discuss the advantages of both methods and give your own opinion.

    One school of thought is that the best approach for child development is parents teaching their children by themselves at home. On the other hand, the second school of thought is that children should attend school for their better development. There is no general consensus over this and both approaches have advantages.

    The foremost advantage of the first approach is that it is undisputed that no one can understand their child better than his/her parents. A child lives with the parents since birth, and parents know each and every aspect of the child. On the other hand, the teacher has to teach the whole class and take care of every student, slow learners and fast learners alike. When parents have one child to teach, they can give him/her their hundred per cent attention. They can schedule the teaching as per their child's pace. Moreover, parents can better look after the child.

Another approach is attending school. This method has its own advantages. In school, a child has to spend his time in class with other children of the same age. He/she start making new friends. They not only talk about studies but also discuss other happenings around them. They share knowledge and information with each other. All the children take part in group activities including extracurricular activities. As a result, their confidence increases in many folds.

As we have observed, both methods have their own advantages. However, according to my opinion it is essential for children to attend school. This way, school and parents share the responsibility of overall development of the child.

13. **Some people believe that the good leaders are born, whereas others hold the opinion that leadership qualities can be obtained during the life. Discuss.**

It is commonly believed that great leaders are born to be a leader. However, it is also considered by some that good leadership attributes can be learned in life. I fully advocate for the latter statement because I believe experience is the best teacher.

To begin with, there is no denying the fact that some people are just naturally blessed with exceptional leadership qualities. For example, the trait theory, which believes that certain people are born or made with some particular qualities that will make them excel in a leadership role. Such people have the ability to inspire others in a variety of ways, which include passion, integrity, courage, a sense of responsibility and creativity. As a result of these attributes they possess, they are considered to make themselves a born leader.

On the other hand, leaders are made, not born. Firstly, behavioural theories believe that people can become leaders through the process of teaching, learning, and observation. Thus we can definitely agree that with, learning and experience one can be a good leader. Secondly, the transformation leadership theory states that an individual can obtain leadership qualities by interacting with others and creating a solid relationship that results in a high percentage of trust. This will later lead to an increase of motivation, both intrinsic and extrinsic, in both leaders and followers. Finally, the trait theory was refuted due to the shortfalls in the analysis which categorically states that no individual is born with such trait.

In conclusion, although some folks still argue that leaders are born naturally with such leadership qualities, I am of the opinion that leadership is a set of skills that can be learned by training, perception, practice and experience.

14. **Some people think that all university students should study whatever they like. Others believe that they should only be allowed to study subjects that will be useful in the future, such as those related to science and technology.**

    Discuss both these views and give your own opinion.

    People have different views about how much choice students should have with regard to what they can study at university. **While some argue that** it would be better for students to be forced into certain key subject areas, **I am of the opinion that** everyone should be able to study the course of their choice.

    There are various reasons why people believe that universities should only offer subjects that will be useful in the future. They may assert that university courses like medicine, engineering and information technology are more likely to be beneficial than certain art degrees. **From a personal perspective,** it can be argued that these courses provide more job opportunities, career progression, better salaries, and therefore an improved quality of life for students who opt them. **On the other hand,** by forcing people to choose particular university subjects, governments can ensure that any knowledge and skill gaps in the economy are adequately covered. For instance, a focus on technology in higher education could lead to new inventions, economic growth, and greater future prosperity.

    In spite of these arguments, I am of the opinion that university students should be free to choose their preferred areas of study because society and economy will benefit more if the students are passionate about what they are learning. **Besides,** nobody can really predict which areas of knowledge will be most useful to society and economy in the future.,

    In conclusion, although it might seem sensible for universities to focus only on the most useful subjects, **I have an insight to support the fact that liberty should be given to students to study subjects of their choice.**

15. **Some people prefer to spend their lives doing the same things and avoiding change. Others, however, think that change is always a good thing.**

    Discuss both these views and give your own opinion

    It is rightly said and believed that, change is a law of nature and it always happens for the good. The statement reflects the opinion of two ideologies. That some people always do the same thing throughout their entire life, whereas others try to learn something new for a change. I am of the opinion that change is always good, and doing things repeatedly may lead to a monotonous life.

    There are some valid reasons why some people feel the need to make significant changes in their lives from time to time. Any new situation can be a learning opportunity and person grows from it. Moreover, it is a phycology of a daring person to accept or change the circumstances for his progress. It can be related to their personal or professional life. Another additional benefit of doing new things is that it makes the person innovative and helps in developing problem solving techniques. Moreover it also helps in moulding his overall personality by opening his mind towards new experiences...

    On the other hand, some people keep on doing the same things repeatedly. This may cause monotony in the work that they are doing, and eventually makes them lose their interest which affects the efficiency and the outcomes. The productivity of a person is hugely affected, which later leads to frustration and, subsequently, a person starts questioning his own capabilities. Such type of people are always insecure in life which has effect on their decision making.

    To conclude with, i strongly believe that change is something that is a basic requirement for a healthy lifestyle as it prevents a person form becoming dull. If one continues to lead a life in which there is no change it would make a person frustrated and would also effect his personality.

16. **Some people believe that school children should not be given homework by their teachers, whereas others argue that homework plays an important role in the education of children.**

Discuss both of these views and give your own opinion.

Homework is a revisional task which is assigned after classroom study. Opinion differ as to whether or not school children should be given homework. While there are some strong arguments against assigning homework, I still believe that it is a necessary aspect of education and the growth of a child. The statement is divided into two different ideologies. Some research scholars believe that the benefits of homework outrages its disadvantages because homework makes a student hardworking and also develops the concentration in studies. Children learn to be self dependent and creative enough to solve the problems creatievely. Even long sitting hours also improves their overall performance.

Another school of thought is of opinion that homework should not be assigned it is because homework is considered as a burden to which children start developing repulsion towards their studies. The level of boredom creates monotony and children start avoiding their studies. Moreover, long sitting hours causes obesityand they also loose interest in outdoor sports.

In spite of the above arguments, I support the view that homework has an important role to play in the schooling of children. The main benefit of homework is that it encourages independent learning and problem solving, as children are challenged to work through tasks alone and at their own pace. In doing so, students must apply the knowledge that they have learnt in the classroom.. In my view, it is important for children to develop independent studying habits, because it prepares them to work alone as adults.

In conclusion, homework certainly has its drawbacks, but I believe that the benefits outweigh them in the long term.

17. **Discuss the positive and negative impacts of an information revolution through mass media.**

Media is a direct source of information and entertainment. It is a public voice in a democratic society. Hence it is a helpline to provide justice to the people. It is generally of two types: electronic and print. Both are very effective, but electronic is very popular. On the other hand, mass media is a wider term and very popular. With the advancement of technology, it includes all the different sources of information, like television, newspaper, social media and any information through satellite.

The statement is clearly segregated into two different ideologies. Discussing about its merits and demerits, it is evident that technology with its optimum usage of information cannot be discouraged. So, it has many advantages. Mass media helps in reducing the crime, opening the scams and also creating fear factor in the mind of criminals. It also helps in providing complete information which results in making a public opinion. It is believed that social media spreads the news like a forest fire, which creates awareness in society regarding what is happening around the world. This subsequently provides awareness to the citizens of the country about their fundamental rights and duties. It contributes to society as it throws light on social evils, malpractices and policies of the government.

Expanding the statement and analysing its demerits, it clearly indicates that mass media has just a handful of negative impressions on society. It sometimes intrudes in the privacy of an individual by making it public. It drives the public away from reality, as the larger section of society forms its opinion on the basis of what is portrayed on the television.

To recapitulate, mass media plays a positive role and responsibility towards society. Accordingly, there should be a vigilance agency to put a strict check on its misuse. Fake news or information that deliberately misleads and deceive the public should be strictly discouraged and strict action should be taken against the journalists or the people involved.

18. **Prices of fuels should be increased. This will solve the problems of environmental hazards. What is your opinion?**

Environmental concern is a seriou issue that are directly related with the pollution. The categories of pollution geographically differ depending on human activities or depletion of resources. It can be air, water, noise, soil or thermal pollution. It is basically a contamination of the environment that depletes the ozone layer and produces noxious gases which causes open threat for the survival of living beings.

Some individuals believe that raising the cost of fuel is the most effective method to solve the world's environmental problems. While I accept that this policy is good to some extent, I believe that it is not the best solution because there are much better measures to reduce environmental issues.

It might be good idea to increase the price of the fuel such as coal, petrol and gas because of some reasons. Firstly, by making it more costly to purchase fuel, government can deter people from using personal vehicles. For instance, if gasoline is more expensive, people will start using public transport rather than driving a car or riding a motorbike, resulting in reduction of CO_2 emission, which is responsible for global warming and climatic change. Secondly, the decrease in the demand of the fuel as a result of high price would lead in the minimization of natural resources exploitation which reduces the problem of waste disposal in such industries. Lastly, as the cost of the fuel is higher, people might use them much more efficiently.

However, I am of the opinion that, there are much better methods to deal with the environmental problems. The first solution is that the government should spend more money on conducting research and developing technology to use renewable energy resources including wind, solar and tidal energy instead of natural resources. By doing this, people can reduce energetic burden on nature. The second solution is to have stricter punishments for environmental criminals. For example, people who have been accused of environmental degradation should be required to pay huge fine or receive a prison sentence. This makes individuals more likely to respect the law, and environmental issues can be limited. Additionally, the government should launch programs or run advertising campaigns to raise people awareness about conserving nature.

To recapitulate, I believe apart from increasing the price of fuel, there are more effective ways to protect the environment. In this context both society as well government plays an essential role. Discussing the role of the government, what needs to be done is that government should frame strict policies and laws against the offenders and impose penalties on those who are found guilty of degrading the environment. Apart from this people should also understand the importance of keeping the environment clean and healthy.

19. **In some countries around the world, voting is compulsory. Do you agree with the notion of compulsory voting? If voting is compulsory in democratic society, what conclusions can we draw about the nature of democracy?**

Voting is a process to express the opinion and favour an ideology. Under the constitution of our country, voting is a fundamental right of every citizen, because it's a regulating body to govern the country under strict laws. It is the highest form of democracy in which the public participates to elect the desired candidate. Casting a vote is a serious responsibility. which can be done by every individual above 18 years old.,

I agree with the statement and support the logic in favour of it. The right to vote is a direct link between authorities and masters. It is a way that people can express their consent. An elected candidate comes under pressure and works for the welfare of society. Deadlines are given, and performance is judged by the public., The process of voting is based on moral and ethical grounds, which makes the society fearless. Voting is anonymous, and the identities of the voters are concealed.

Analysing the statement further, voting is the heart of democracy. As long as people are given the chance to vote and to choose their representatives, their stance on social and political issues, then democracy is working. That is why it is essential to ensure that every eligible voter is registered and will exercise their right of suffrage, because if not it defeats the purpose of democracy. A society that makes voting hard for people is pretentious democratic society. The government should legislate laws that make voting much easier for all citizens, particularly those unrepresented groups whose voices are often unheard in the halls of government offices.

To recapitulate, voting is the right of every citizen living in a democratic country, but strict business tendencies and election commissions should work hard to observe that there is no corruption in the system of voting. Malpractices like capturing and corruption in the election system should be highly punishable, and awareness among people should be created so that every citizen of the country understands the importance of casting his vote. The progress of the country is dependent on the people who are elected by the citizens themselves. They become the face and the voice of every individual and represent the country on behalf of the citizens.

20. **What is the cause of water shortage? How should water be preserved and utilized?**

Natural resources are non-renewable resources. This is the biggest gift of nature. They help to regulate the ecosystem's air, water and sunlight. Coal and petroleum are some natural resources that help to sustain life. Water is an important natural resource, which creates survival conditions for living beings.

Water scarcity is the lack of fresh water resources to meet water demand. It affects every continent and is marked as one of the major global risks for the potential generations. The increasing world population, improving living standards, changing consumption patterns, and expansion of irrigated agriculture are the main driving forces for the rising global demand of water. Climatic change, such as altered weather-patterns including droughts, floods, deforestation, increased pollution, green house gases, and wasteful use of water can cause insufficient supply of water. Thus all causes of water scarcity are related to human interference with the water cycle.

Water scarcity has many negative impacts on the environment, including lakes, rivers and other fresh water resources. The resulting water overuse that is related to water scarcity, often located in areas of irrigation agriculture, harms the environment in several ways including salinity, nutrient pollution etc.

Explaining further, there is a shortage of fresh and clean water. Due to the dumping of industrial waste and various other human activities, the water bodies are getting contaminated. This is subsequently disrupting the whole system, as such water is not fit for consumption. It is the duty of every individual to save water for future generations. The government should impose penalties to aid it in checking water wastage. Recycling water is a good option to save fresh water. It can be used in industries or households.

To recapitulate, water is the only natural resource that makes the earth a fit planet for survival. Methods like rainwater harvesting and recycled wastewater should be encouraged, as it allows reducing scarcity and easing pressures on groundwater and natural water bodies. Improving water infrastructure must be a priority, as water conservation and efficiency are key components of sustainable water management. Last but not the least, education is critical to solve the water crisis. In fact, in order to cope with future water scarcity, it is necessary to educate people to use water efficiently and make them aware about the importance of water and the impact that they and the coming generations would face, if they do not address this issue seriously.

Some Practice Tasks

1. Law changes the behaviour of the society. Agree or disagree?

<u>Intro:</u> Law is a legal protection given to the citizens of the country. The objective behind the law is to provide safety and security to the citizens. It also helps in creating peace and harmony among the communities. The law stands on the platform of equality. Everyone is equal in the eyes of law. Moreover, punishments are given by the law after a fair trial. This corrects the behaviour of society.

BP 1 →

Agree

1. It creates a fear factor in the minds of the criminals.

2. The law corrects the attitude by teaching discipline to the common man.

3. The fear of punishment acts as a deterrent, which instils the feeling of fear in the minds of the criminals.

4. It helps maintain order in the society.

BP 2 →

Agree

1. Law makes a society civilized.

2. Law helps in regulating social, political and economic machinery.

3. Law always provides protection, safety and security to the common man. And the fear of law is always stronger, which conducts the behaviour of the individuals.

Conclusion:

1. Strict implementation of the law makes a country progressive.

2. The purpose is to provide justice and reduce the feeling of revenge.

3. It is the highest authority to correct behaviour and teach lessons, so it should be respected.

4. Law-abiding citizens always contribute towards the betterment of the society.

2. Old people enjoy old age homes. Do you agree or disagree?

Or

Some people believe that old people should be sent to old age homes. Agree or disagree.

Intro: Old people are physically and biologically weak and need constant support and care. Old age homes are government or non-government organizations that promise to take care of senior citizens. It is undeniable that old people are the pillars of society. They are highly experienced and wise decision makers. And it is only physical age that becomes a big hurdle in their working.

↓

BP 1 ⟶

Agree:

1. Due to heavy industrialization and modernization, the trend of migration is increasing.

2. This is due to the impact of global culture, which is causing the structure of families to change from joint to nuclear.

3. Per-capita income as well as competition is increasing and people are running short of time and space.

4. Senior citizens that are destitute or are unable in settling with their respective families can easily stay in homes meant for old people.

5. Main benefits of these homes are their staff's good behaviour, wholesome food as well as good services.

BP 2 ⟶

1. There are facilities like medication, recreation and meditation workshops in old age homes.

2. This is a trend that started in developed nations.

3. It is now becoming popular across the globe.

Conclusion

1. Old people are the most respected section of society.

2. They have served the family and the nation.

3. It should be the top priority of the government to provide maximum comforts and securities to the senior citizens.

4. Youngsters should offer their volunteer services to teach the latest technology to old people.

5. This will keep them busy, healthy, updated and self-dependent.

6. These play roles of safe haven for senior citizens who have got nobody to take care of them or have not got a place to stay. Residents here get an ambience of complete family. They are given unique sense of friendship as well as security here. It becomes a place for them to share their sorrows as well as joys.

Task 2: Spider Chart Practice

1. **Some people believe that environmental problems are too big to be solved whereas others oppose the opinion. Discuss the statement and give reasons.**

INTRO → Environmental problems are serious concerns that contaminate the environment by depleting the ozone layer and emitting noxious gases. These problems are directly related with different types of pollutions which causes health problems and even disturbs the ecosystem with sudden change in climatic conditions. Such problems need to be handled at the war footing.

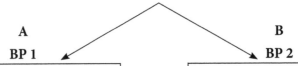

A		**B**
BP 1		**BP 2**

BP 1	BP 2
The people of developing and underdeveloped countries believe the problem <u>is too big.</u>	The people of developed countries believe the problem <u>is not too big.</u>
Reasons	**Reasons**
1. Resources are minimum	1. Resaources are enough
2. People are deprived of basic amenities	2. There is no corruption
3. Awareness is less	3. Public money is used for the public benefits
4. There are no recycling plants.	4. Literacy rate is high
5. Garbage is littered at public places which causes pollution	5. People prefer to use eco-friendly products

Conclusion:

1. The green belt area should be wide-spread.

2. Both the government and the public should join hands to solve the problem.

3. Sustainable development should be encouraged.

Writing Task Notes

(With the help of these notes you can make the following answers)

Sports

Sports are the physical and mental activities that keep the body fit and fine. They also increase stamina and de-stress by providing complete relaxation to the mind and body of a person. Sports are of two types: indoor and outdoor. But the purpose of both is to provide complete entertainment. Nowadays, the trend of international sports is multiplying rapidly, and every country is becoming conscious about its expenditure on sports.

Benefits of Sports

- They have tremendous health benefits, like it helps to maintain weight, lowering the risk of heart diseases, reducing blood pressure and reducing stress.
- They teach discipline, team spirit and a feeling of brotherhood.
- They reduce social evils like drug addiction.
- They occupy the youth of the country by inculcating in them the feeling of patriotism.
- Sports promote tourism.
- They generate job opportunities.
- They help to keep the mind and body of a person healthy and fit.
- Sports contribute to bringing name and fame to the country.

Importance of Sports Among Children

- Sports develop the overall personality of children.
- During the physical education period, awareness of health, diet and exercise is created.

- Sports are considered to be very healthy and recreational activity among children.

- They learn team spirit, discipline and cultural tolerance. This makes them a better citizen.

- Some sports can be taken as a future career for the children.

- In school, sports break the monotony of studies and give freshness to develop creativity.

Importance of Sports for Adults

- During this age, sports are not taken as career.

- They are pure entertainment.

- They are a very good form of exercise.

- Adults make sports clubs in colonies or localities, which keeps them united.

- Relations and circles among adults expand.

- They reduce stress, and work becomes better.

Rural Sports Should Be Promoted

- These are some sports that are played without any observation and without any rules.

- They differ from state to state.

- Sports have an age-old history.

- They were invented keeping in mind the interest, ability and even the culture of the city.

- Rural sports unite not only youngsters but many sections of society.

- Sports fairs are organized at global level and some countries make it religious and traditional festivals.

- A village is geographically a small area and sports unite it very well.

- It is believed that rural sports reduce social evils and crime.

Dangerous Sports (Adventurous) Should Not Be Banned

- Adventurous sports like sky diving, bungee jumping or river rafting should not be banned because they are a platform for talented people to exhibit their talent.

- It is not a compulsion to perform such sports.

- Adventurous sports are a complete thrill for the performer and the viewer.

- They generate tourism.

- They make the country and individuals famous.

- Even sports like boxing and wrestling that are considered violent should not be banned, because they are played without ill-will (jealously).

- The talent of an individual in sports should be respected and rewarded.

- Adventurous sports reduce fear.

Computer Games Should Be Encouraged Among Children

- They increase mental abilities.

- A child learns time management.

- They develop an interest in graphics.

- Computer games are becoming the most popular indoor games.

- They are very entertaining and educative.

- They polish skill and also helps in developing interest in computers.

- The future of the world is standing on digitalization and computer games are a good revolution.

Government Should Take Serious Steps to Promote the Sports

- Jobs should be generated.

- It should ensure the safety and security of a sportsmen related to his future.

- Facilities like playgrounds, techniques and a healthy diet should be provided for better performance.

- Technology should be introduced.

- Talent search programmes should be encouraged to uplift and motivate young sportsmen.

- Equal opportunities for both genders should be created.

- Sponsorships should be arranged for all games.

- Corruption like match-fixing should be penalised.

- Stadiums and live telecasts should be made to involve maximum audience for entertainment.

- No political parties should interfere in sports. This will reduce international stress, and countries will become closer.

Questons:

Question 1: Some people believe that sports teach children how to compete, while others believe that children learn how to work in a team with others, rather than against them.

Discuss both views and give your opinion.

Question 2: Ensuring that children have regular physical exercise should be the responsibility of parents, and therefore schools should not waste valuable time having sports lessons as part of the curriculum.

To what extent do you agree?

Question 3: Many countries apply to host international sporting competitions, such as the Olympics, but only one is chosen each time.

What are benefits of a country hosting an international sports competition?

Do you think the advantages outweigh the disadvantages?

Question 4: Some people think that companies should provide employees with exercise time during the day.

What is your opinion about this?

Question 5: With an increase in health problems such as obesity, stress, etc., some people think universities should make sports a compulsory module in all degree courses.

To what extent do you agree?

Question 6: Professional sportspersons are often idolized by young children. Some people think that they, therefore, have a responsibility to be good role models at all times.

Do you agree with this?

Question 7: Some people think that sports involving violence, such as boxing and martial arts, should be banned from TV as well as from international sporting competitions.

To what extent do you agree?

Questions

1. Benefits of Sports:

Sports give name and fame to a country. Therefore, they cannot be ignored under any condition. Discuss and give your opinion?

2. Sports Promote Tourism:

Sports are considered a binding factor at the international level. Do you agree or disagree?

3. Rural Sports Should Be Promoted:

Sports are equal for every caste, colour and region. Therefore, their promotion in remote areas is highly important. Discuss and give your opinion?

4. Computer Games Should Be Encouraged Among Children:

Some people believe computer games cause distraction, while others oppose the statement. Discuss and give your opinion.

BUILDINGS

Innovation in architecture is, without a doubt, extremely important, but preserving and restoring old buildings is even more important. Buildings can be of various categories; they can be historical, religious or even monumental, but all buildings have their own importance, and sometimes important buildings make the place very famous.

Historical Buildings Should Not Be Torn Down

➢ They reflect the culture and the tradition.

➢ They have intrinsic value.

➢ They are a referral point for the research scholars.

➢ They give a comparative study of past and present.

➢ They have historical significance. Their restoration is of utmost importance because they are reflections of our history.

➢ Historical buildings are tourist hubs.

➢ People from all over the world visit such buildings.

➢ They become common attractions for educational trips among schools and colleges.

➢ They help promote tourism.

Benefits of Tall Buildings

➢ It is the optimum utilization of the land.

➢ It serves the best purpose where the population is high.

➢ Many tasks can be performed in such buildings.

➢ Tall buildings or skyscrapers are examples of developed countries.

➢ As the inevitable result of growing population and intensifying urbanization, high rise residential towers have become more prevalent in many cities, replacing vast areas of vernacular houses.

> ➤ Such buildings are beautiful and the pride of a country. They are more about power and prestige status.

> ➤ They provide almost every facility, so nowadays, old buildings are replaced by modern architecture.

Questions

Q1. Some people believe that, due to overpopulation, there is a shortage of space, so old and big buildings should be torn down. Do you agree or disagree?

Q2. Historical buildings are the pride of a country. Should they be torn down and replaced by new ones?

Q3. Discuss the benefits of living in a flat.

Q4. Modern buildings and skyscrapers are becoming highly popular. Discuss the statement and give your opinion.

ANIMALS

Question:

Animals are commonly used by scientists to conduct various experiments. This causes trouble, discomfort and pain to the animals. Do you agree or disagree?

Introduction

Animals are a beautiful creation of nature. They play an important role in human life. They all behave according to their breed. They can be categorized as wild and domestic animals. For ages, animals have contributed to maintain the balance in nature by maintain the food chain. On the other hand, animals that humans have used for food, labour and companionship over countless generations have helped society advance to the point it has reached today. Therefore, it would be a sheer injustice to kill, hurt or torture animals for personal benefits.

Experiments Should Be Conducted

➤ The anatomy of animals is similar to the human body, so it gives the best results.

➤ Experiments give positive results which help in progress of medical science, advancement of hospitals, medicines and diagnostics centres are a result of such experimentation.

➤ Experiments are conducted on fast breeding animals.

➤ This does not disturb the food chain.

➤ Animal scientists work with farmers to improve animal breeding, diseases and nutrition.

Animals Should Not Be Tortured or Used for Personal Benefit

➤ They are living beings.

➤ They are helpless.

> ➤ People must not use animals for their necessity. For instance, using them for entertainment business, killing them for clothes etc. is inhuman. These activities not only hurt the animals but also destroy and disturb the nature of balance.

> ➤ Taking out the skin and the organs of animals and leaving them to die in pain is a punishable offence.

> ➤ Violation of animal rights like hunting or caging is against the law.

> ➤ Animals always help to maintain a balance in the ecosystem. They act as scavengers.

Zoo (Sanctuaries Should Be Encouraged)

> ➤ A zoo is an open area where animals are kept in natural habitats.

> ➤ They are provided with open space and complete medical facilities.

> ➤ Endangered species are very well protected from hunting and caging.

> ➤ The animal kingdom needs to have a separate area because they cannot fit in human society.

Animals Should Be Taken Care of:

> ➤ In experimentation, they should not be cut and torn.

> ➤ Experiments should be conducted under the supervision of law.

> ➤ Brutality towards animals should be strictly prohibited.

> ➤ It would otherwise disturb the food chain.

Questions

Q1. Some people use animals for their personal benefits. Discuss the statement and give your opinion.

Q2. Torturing animals should be strongly punished. Do you agree or disagree?

Q3. Animals help propagate the food chain. Discuss the reasons for the extinction of the animals and provide solutions.

Q4. Animals should be kept in zoos and sanctuaries. This protects animal rights. Do you agree or disagree?

QUESTION: Success is only due to hard work. Luck does not make a person successful or unsuccessful. Do you agree or disagree?

Hard work is the key to success. To yield fruitful results, it is essential that one is fully dedicated towards his goals and ambitions in life. When a person focuses wholeheartedly, no one can stop him from reaching the heights of success. On the other hand, luck is a metaphysical force and an unforeseen factor, which is difficult to rely on.

In my opinion, hard work is the only key to success because it makes a person confident and self-dependent. There are different steps and channels to work hard, only then, the targets and the goals can be achieved. Hard work makes a person mature and knowledgeable. It gives an experience which is beneficial for the competitive world. It also provides a strong sense of motivation which develops the creative skills.

Another school of thought is of the opinion that luck plays a major role. It goes without saying that luck is a reward a person gets without effort. But the level of predictability is low, and this makes a person coward, superstitious and laid back. He loses his faith in himself. Moreover, it is a step towards negativity and laziness. It is strongly believed that every person has to undergo testing times, and complete belief on luck leads to certain failure.

To recapitulate, in my opinion God helps those who help themselves. Hard work in the right direction with strong willpower makes a person lucky. If there is clarity of mind with no confusion, then hard work always pays off. Difficult situations are the lessons that teach us to never give up during difficult times.

ADVERTISEMENT

Some people believe that advertisements are deceptive. On the other hand, they increase product sales. Discuss and give your opinion.

To paraphrase, advertisement is a process used to multiply sales. It is an important strategy of marketing products or a message to promote sales, services or even ideas. Advertising is communicated through various mass media including traditional mass media such as newspapers, radios, televisions and magazines, and new media such as Facebook, Twitter and various other social networking sites. The actual presentation of a message by using any of such modes is called advertisement. Keeping in mind the categories, publicity of the advertisement differs from place to place. Even mouth-to-mouth publicity is very popular and one of the most effective techniques to sell the product.

Advertisement Enhances the Sales of the Product...

1. It creates desire which leads to demand and in turn leads to supply.

2. It is a practical change that promises hefty profits to the organization.

3. Advertisement creates awareness.

4. It helps introduce or launch new products in the market.

5. Advertisement, along with a strategy and different techniques, captures the market.

6. In the past, there were less advertisements and people enjoyed purchasing local products, whereas nowadays the international market is giving very tough competition, which is not possible without advertisements.

7. It helps in expansion of the market.

Some Advertisements Are Deceptive

1. They make false promises.

2. Features are not clearly projected. They offer heavy discounts and misleading schemes with flowery language which confuses the customers

3. Role models and celebrities attract the masses to make the product popular.

4. Another limitation of advertisements is that big companies have an undue advantage with them of having a higher budget for advertisements, whereas local manufacturers or small companies do not have any budget, which results in bigger companies advertising and selling those products that are of lower quality than local manufacturers product. Hence, in a way, advertisements kill competition and give larger companies an unfair advantage over smaller companies.

5. Advertisement can be misleading, and not all products or services which are advertised are good, and hence, in a way, advertisements give the wrong impression in the minds of consumers, leading them to purchase the advertised inferior-quality product or service.

Advertisements in School Should Be Limited

1. Children are immature and get easily manipulated.

2. They are the soft target.

3. By nature, they are very innocent and demand popular products as a sign of prestige.

4. Harmful products like fast food, chocolates or soft drinks should not be promoted.

To recapitulate, advertisement is the need of an hour and is necessary for promotion of any sort of business. . Survival is not possible in trading without advertising, but there should be a vigilance agency to check misleading advertisements that could negatively affect people's health or future.

(Same intro and conclusion for both essays.)

Questions

Q:1 Violence in the media promotes violence in society.

To what extent do you agree?

Q:2 Most people think that the truth should be objective, rather than subjective, when it comes to the news.

Do you think all news is true?

What is the function of a newspaper?

Q:3 More and more newspapers and news channels are using photographs to support their news articles and stories. Some people think that photographs are not a reliable source of news while others consider photographs to be irrefutable.

Discuss both sides and give your opinion.

Q:4 The majority of news being reported is bad news, such as wars, famines, accidents and crime.

Why do you think that is?

Do you think the news should be a balance of both good and bad news?

Q:5 In the last few decades there have been more and more cases of famous people being hounded by the press. Some people think that famous people in the media have no right to privacy.

To what extent do you agree?

Q:6 People in the limelight have the responsibility to set an example for others with their good behaviour.

Do you agree?

Q:7 With the development of the media online, there is no future for the radio.

To what extent do you agree?

Q:8 Watching TV is a waste of time for children.

Do you agree or disagree?

Q:9 Companies spend millions each year on advertising online, in magazines and on billboards. These adverts can encourage people to buy goods that they do not really need.

What are the positive and negative effects of consumerism?

Q:10 One of the prime times for advertising on TV is when children get back from school. Some people think that advertisements aimed at children should not be allowed.

What is your opinion?

Q:11 Many people buy products they do not really need and replace old products with new ones unnecessarily.

Why do people buy things they do not really need?

Do you think this is a good thing?

Q:12 Many people think that fast food companies should not be allowed to advertise, while others believe that all companies should have the right to advertise.

What is your opinion?

GOVERNMENT

QUESTION: Some people think that the government is wasting money on art and that this money could be better spent elsewhere.

To what extent do you agree with this view?

Art and craft is the reflection of the culture and heritage of a country. It is an age-old expression to express history, religion or personality through statues. A country always promotes its traditions. On the other hand, spending money always depends on the economic structure of the nation.

In my opinion, to get the basic clarity regarding this, it is important to understand that, in underdeveloped countries, the priorities are quite different. The people are deprived of basic amenities such as schools, hospitals, transport system and medical facilities. People are homeless and suffers from corruption, poverty and unemployment. Under such conditions, they will never welcome the idea that the government should spend public money on art to beautify the city.

Explaining further, it is a welcome policy to spend money on art, because developed countries have enough resources to make their citizens comfortable. There is complete security of job and health. Surplus money can be invested to beautify the city. It is important because it attracts tourism and the country gets benefits such as social and economic progress.

On the whole, the government should spend the money according to their level of affordability. Spending money on art is a positive development but only when people are healthy and are enjoying the basic amenities of their life.

HANDS-ON

➤ Transport

    I. With an increase in the number of privately owned vehicles, roads are becoming more congested.

    What measures can both government and individuals take to deal with this situation?

    II. The impact that the growing demand for more flights has had on the environment is a major concern for many countries. Some people believe that one way to limit the number of people travelling by air is to increase tax on flights.

    To what extent do you think this could solve the problem?

    III. Some people think it should be compulsory for people to retake their driving test every 5 years.

    What are the advantages and disadvantages of doing this?

    IV. One way of solving congestion on the roads is to increase tax on private vehicles.

    How could this alleviate congestion?

    What other measures can you suggest to deal with congestion in cities?

    V. Some people think that in order to deal with problem of congestion in the cities, privately owned vehicles should be banned in city centres while others consider it to be an unrealistic solution.

    Discuss both sides and give your opinion.

    VI. A poor infrastructure hinders underdeveloped nations from progressing and modernising. Some people think this should be the first problem tackled by foreign aid.

    To what extend do you agree with this opinion?

    VII. One way to solve the problem of congestion in cities is to build sky-trains which run overhead, rather than on or under the ground.

    What are the advantages and disadvantages of using this solution to solve congestion?

TOURISM

I. As a result of tourism and the increasing number of people travelling, there is a growing demand for flights.

What problems does this have on the environment?

What measures can be taken to solve this problem?

II. Some people believe that to protect local culture, tourism should be banned in some areas, whereas others think that change is inevitable and banning tourism will have no benefits.

Discuss both sides and give your opinion.

III. As a result of tourism, many historical sites and buildings are being damaged beyond repair.

What could be done to prevent this?

IV. Some people think that when they travel to different cultures they should adapt the local practices and customs.

To what extend do you agree?

V. The development of tourism contributed to English becoming the most prominent language in the world. Some people think this will lead to English becoming the only language to be spoken globally.

What are the advantages and disadvantages to having one language in the world.

WORK

I. Completing university education is thought by some to be the best way to get a good job. On the other hand, some people think that getting experience and developing soft skills is more important.

Discuss both sides and give your opinion.

II. First impressions are important. Some people think that doing well in interviews is the key to securing a job.

To what extent do you agree?

III. Finding job satisfaction is considered a luxury in many developing countries. Why do you think that is?

Do you think job satisfaction is important?

IV. Famous stars and some professionals can command a very high salary. Some people think that it is fair because salaries should be based on people's gifts and talents. Others, however, believe that a person's salary should be based on their contribution to society.

Discuss both sides and give your opinion.

V. Many children are encouraged by their parents to get a part-time job in their free time.

What are the advantages and disadvantages to children of doing so?

VI. In many developing countries, there is an increasing movement of workers from rural areas into cities.

Why do you think this happens?

What problem can it cause?

VII. In some developing countries, it is difficult to get good teachers to work in rural areas, which can have a negative impact on the education of children in those rural communities.

Why do you think good teachers do not want to work in rural areas in developing countries?

What could solve this problem?

VIII. Having a good university degree guarantees people a good job.

To what extent do you agree?

Polishing Practice Test

EDUCATION

Question 1: Education develops the overall personality and helps in proper utilization of resources? Do you agree or disagree?

Question 2: Education is the responsibility of the government; primary education should be state responsibility. Discuss the statement and give your opinion.

Question 3: Techniques of education are changing with the passage of time? What steps should be taken to introduce quality education? Expand the statement and give your views.

Question 4: Certain courses in education should be mandatory at primary level whereas the major choices should depended on personal interest. Do you agree or disagree?

Question 5: A university should guide the student regarding its utilization in the professional field otherwise education without job has no meaning? Do you agree or disagree?

Question 6: The trend of international education is multiplying rapidly. What should be done to improve the quality of education in the native country? Give suggestions.

Question 7: Primary education is more important than colleges? Do you agree or disagree?

Question 8: Traditional is still considered to be the easiest technique of simplifying the concepts? Do you agree or disagree?

Question 9: In University, is education practical or traditional? Give your opinion.

Question 10: Some people think that a yearly break between high school and college or university is essential. Do you agree or disagree?

INTRODUCTION

About University

A university is an institution of higher education and research. Universities typically provide undergraduate and postgraduate education. An important idea in this definition is the notion of academic freedom, which enables the students to choose their career according to their passion and interest.

About Education

Education is a lifelong process of learning and gaining knowledge. It grooms the personality and creates job opportunities. It is the process of facilitating learning, or acquisition of knowledge, skills, values, beliefs and habits. Education primarily takes place under the guidance of teachers. Education can take place in formal and informal settings.

Formal education is commonly divided into stages: preschool, kindergarten, primary school, secondary school, college and then university. On the other hand, **informal education** is a general term of education. It encompasses students' interests. It has no set of formulas or guidelines.

Types of Education

➤ Traditional Education

- It is a psychological application that is imparted according to the mental ability of the candidate.
- It is personal with high level of interaction.
- It is expensive as human resources are directly involved.
- In this, simplification of the concepts is prime motive.

➤ Online Education

- It has audio-visual impact.
- Increases interest and retention.
- Time saving.

- Energy saving.

- It promises accuracy.

- It stands on the platform of international up gradation.

- A student can study and work simultaneously.

- Global education.

Benefits to the Country

The country will be technically advanced, which will be a gateway for industrialization, modernization, global job opportunities, social and economic standards, high per capita income, international trade, regulation of law and order.

Demerits of an Uneducated Person

- Unemployment.

- Extortion and kidnapping.

- Lack of awareness regarding fundamental rights.

- Inability to increase creative skills.

- Increased terrorism.

- Lawlessness in society.

- Increase in the population.

Demerits

- When distribution of degree is higher than job opportunities, it causes an imbalance in available resources and multiplies the crime rate.

- Brain drain.

Suggestions/Conclusion

- The government should spend money to improve the quality of education at the primary level.

- Latest techniques should be introduced.

- International education should be promoted.

- Variety of course combinations should be introduced which are related to the jobs.

- Easy loans should be provided for higher education.

- State should take the responsibility to increase the rate of literacy.

Benefits of Continution of Studies

- It does not break momentum.

- It develops the creative skills.

- Candidates become more hardworking and energetic as alluring opportunities lies ahead.

Benefits pf Study Breaks

- A person becomes experienced.

- It develops the practical skills.

- Able to fund own higher studies.

- Research aptitude develops.

- They become more focused and can study better (quality).

page 215 of 312

SCIENCE

Question 1: Science is causing pollution? Agree or disagree.

Question 2: Technology is the output of experiments, facilities should be provided by the government. Otherwise it is a complete waste of resources? Do you agree or disagree.

Question 3: Big cities are enjoying overall progress but they are suffering from number of problems? Discuss the problem in relation with the progress and give us opinion.

Question 4: Unification of culture is multiplying with the advancement but the traditional values are falling rapidly? Do you agree or disagree.

Question 5: Science reduces superstition and increases the level of awareness? Do you agree or disagree.

Question 6: The world is expanding whereas the distances are becoming short. Expand on the statement and give us your opinion.

Question 7: The overall growth can be measured through the living style. Changes are the proof of revolution. Discuss the changes and give suggestions for the problem that occur due to changes.

Question 8: Computers and cell phones are increasing world trade. Some people believe this is the maximum advancement, whereas others are of the opinion that much can be done. Discuss the statement and give us your opinion.

Question 9: Everything handled by technology will make man a machine. This will increase the stress level; whereas others believe it helps organize one's lifestyle. Discuss the statement and give us your opinion.

Question 10: Who is happier? Us or our forefathers? Give us your opinion.

Question 11: Latest technology creates the fear of war. To what extent can you justified the statement?

Question 12: Global warming is a result of experiments. Should experiments be reduced to protect the environment? Suggest the remedies.

Question 13: Technology benefits every field; sports enjoy the most benefits of technology? Discuss the statement with examples?

Question 14: Outlook of the people change within the changing era, others think it is degeneration of society. Discuss the statement and give us opinion?

Introduction

Science is a logical application which produces results by proving the hypothetical statement and conducting the latest experiments. It is a field of innovation where creative skills are acknowledged and it becomes a workshop for the betterment of mankind. Techniques are making the life highly organized, comfortable and competent. It develops international relation and widens the horizon for global vision.

Agree Points

➢ Industrialization

➢ Creating job opportunities

➢ Leading to modernization

- Migration

- Urbanization

- Technology directly uplifts the socioeconomic standard of the society.

- It increases the per capita income and provides employment opportunities even to the weakest segment of society.

- Transportation and communication has created a revolt in the world which has made the world a global village and has helped in increasing the connectivity.

- It creates level of awareness.

Example: Database

Underdeveloped	Developed	Developing
Approx: 30–40%	95–99%	60–70%

Comparative study

Past	Present
1. Technology was not advanced.	1. Highly advanced.
2. Society was confined to a homogeneous culture.	2. Heterogeneous culture
3. Literacy rate was low.	3. Awareness and literacy rate is high.
4. Cultures dominated business.	4. Flexibility for migration.
5. Traditional beliefs were very strong.	5. Interest competition is creating high level of awareness.

Recapitulation

- **Research centres (by govt.)**

- **There should be implementation on talent exchange programs**

- **Technology is a mutual human resource; it is the pride of the country, as well as the index and benchmark to have relations with other countries.**

Suggestion

- Government should promote talent exchange programs in every field. This will create innovative experiments and will work for the betterment of mankind.

- The government should provide facilities and job opportunities to scientists to reduce brain drain.

- Awareness should be created at the primary level.

- Usage of techniques should be common across every age group.

- Workshops should be arranged to teach the techniques to illiterate people.

SPORTS

Question 1: Sports promotes good relations. Agree or disagree.

Question 2: Sports is the profession and the revenue generating sector of the country. Agree or disagree.

Question 3: Sports make better citizens. Explain the statement and give us opinion.

Question 4: The government is spending money on the promotion of games. This is important for the upliftment of the country. Give us your views.

Question 5: The trend of traditional businesses like agriculture is falling, as society is attracted to various sports. Do you agree or disagree?

Question 6: The money earned by the sportsman is justified, so they should not take the commercial breaks. Give us your opinion.

Question 7: The corruption in sports damages the image of the country? What steps should be taken to put a check? Explain? Give us your opinion.

Question 8: Politics should not interfere with sports; otherwise sports would become a part of political machinery. Agree or disagree.

Question 9: Rural games should be given equal importance at international levels as the other games? Do you agree or disagree?

Question 10: Physical education is a technical way to promote the sports. Suggest the steps that should be used for the promotion of games?

Question 11: Equal importance by sponsors should be given to all games. Discuss its benefits with your opinion.

Introduction

Sports are no longer leisurely activities but lucrative professions which have become the prestige of the country. Sports play a very important role in our life as it keeps us healthy and active. Great achievements come our way when we maintain our physical and mental well-being, and sports contributes to our life in a way to maintain good health. They are categorically divided into indoor and outdoor games. It not only exhibits talent but also helps to maintain overall fitness.

Benefits

- Develops travel and tourism.
- Increases job opportunities.
- Promotes cultural fusion.
- Develops the country socially, economically and politically.
- Increases privatization and advertisements.
- Improves coordination and overall personality of an individual.

Qualities of Sportsmen

- Teaches discipline.
- Increases patriotism.
- Team spirit.
- Ethical values.
- Self-sacrifice for the pride of the country.

Disadvantages

The advantages of sports often outweigh the disadvantages. In spite of this, certain disadvantages of sports can be:

- Corruption like match fixing.
- Heavy bidding and misusing the sports for the personal benefits.
- Risk of injury

Steps to Improve the Game

- Security should be provided.
- Qualified professionals should be present instead of honorary members.
- Rural sports should be equally promoted.
- The best way to develop sports at grassroot level is to integrate it as a goal for schools to pursue.

- Sports should be encouraged as a hobby and a profession.

- Tie-ups with foreign bodies who have a vested interest in developing sports.

- Sponsorship should be from the government as well.

- Politics should never be mixed with sports. It should be played as a pure game.

- Increase funds for sports-based firms.

SPEAKING TEST

FORMAT

The table below is a short versioned format of how the speaking test works.

Part	Timing	Content
Introduction	30 seconds	Name, nationality, ID check
Part-1 Interview	3.5–4.5 mins	2 or 3 unrelated, short, simple conversation about your personal preferences or experiences.
Part-2 Cue Card	3–4 mins	1-minute preparation time 1–2 min talk on a topic which draws on your personal experience.
Part-3 Discussion	4–5 mins	A more detailed discussion related to the topic of the cue card in part 2.

MARKING SCHEME

The table below shows how the distribution of the 9 bands is done on the basis of different levels.

Body Language	Fluency/Grammar	Approach
3 bands	3 bands	3 bands
Always stay confident and put appropriate expressions on your face while answering the questions. Sit in a proper position and maintain your poise to get full marks in body language.	Fluency and grammar go hand in hand for the speaking module. You need to be fluent with your answers along with using correct grammar.	The approach of the answer includes the clarity with which you're able to justify the relevancy of your answers. For this part, to score full marks, examples with the statement are a must.

Short Questions

Q1. Could you tell me your full name please?

Sir/Ma'am, my name is … (always mention your full name).

Q2. Do you like your name?

Yes, my name is my identity and was given to me by my parents.

Q3. Can I see your ID?

Yes sure, here it is.

Q4. Are you a student?

Yes, sir/ma'am, I study at…

No, sir/ma'am, I work at…

Q5. Where are you from?

I belong to/hail from…

My hometown is… + (say two lines about it)

Q6. Can I see your passport?

Yes, here it is.

It is my pleasure.

Q7. Describe the area you live in.

I live in a posh colony, where all the facilities like regular supply of electricity and water, and well-maintained parks and roads are provided.

Q8. Why did you choose to live in that area?

Well, my parents live there, so I've lived there since birth.

There are all kinds of facilities available, so I enjoy staying here.

Q9. What kinds of people live in your area?

Most of them are educated, helpful and have the civic sense to not litter in the locality.

Q10. Why do you like this place?

I really like this place because my family lives here, Moreover, almost all the facilities such as transport, hospital and a market are readily available.

Q11. What do you like about your home?

The best thing about my house is that it is spacious and very well ventilated.

Q12. What is your favourite place at home and why?

I love to sit near the balcony of my own room. It relaxes me.

Q13. Which is your favourite colour?

My favourite colour is... *and stability*   *associated with depth*

Moreover, I like different colours according to the season, my mood and *symbolizes trust, loyalty, confidence* occasion. For example, during summers I prefer pastel colours. *truth and faith.*

Q14. Do colours have any special meaning in your country?

Yes. My country is a religious country, and various colours have different meanings. For instance, our own national flag.

Q15. What is the colour of your room?

The colour of my room is...because it reflects light.

Q16. What is easier for you to remember, names or number?

Names are easier for me to remember because they are used regularly and they don't change often.

Q17. Do you like birds?

Yes, they are a symbol of freedom and an important part of ecosystem.

Q18. Do you think birds are important in our life? Why?

Yes, birds are very important in our life because they are an important part of ecosystem and help in maintaining food chain.

Q19. Should people protect birds? Why?

Yes, people should definitely protect birds because they are living beings.

Q20. Do you spend too much money on clothes?

I am a planned shopper and I spend money according to my affordability. But nowadays, branded clothes are expensive, so I sometimes spend more money because I like higher-quality clothes.

Q21. Do you judge a person on the basis of his clothes?

Sorry, (no) I don't judge a person on the basis of his/her clothes. It is an individualistic choice that varies from person to person.

Q22. What is your opinion about fashion?

I believe that fashion updates and upgrades society and defines who we are as individuals.

Q23. What is the negative side of fashion?

Although there is no negative side to fashion, when it becomes unaffordable it can lead to crime.

Q24. Do you like flowers?

Flowers reduce pollution, beautify areas and can be a good gift. And I have a beautiful garden full of flowers in my house.

Q25. What types of flowers are there in your country?

My country enjoys all four seasons, and almost every type of flower is available throughout the year.

Q26. What is the importance of flowers in your society?

Flowers are very important in my society as they are used for various purposes like decorations, gifts and worshipping.

Q27. What kinds of flowers have a special meaning? Why?

Flowers like rose and lotus have special meanings. The rose is a symbol of love, while the lotus stands for purity.

Q28. What are the benefits of living near a river?

We all know that every civilization starts near a river. Moreover, it keeps the temperature moderate, and some people visit river as picnic spots.

Q29. What are the drawbacks of living near the water?

Living near the river can have various drawbacks, like a constant fear of flooding, which can cause the loss of life and property, and many water-borne diseases can occur.

Q30. What is the most common way to get a job now?

Well, these days I would say the most common way to get a job is through websites like monster.com.

Q31. How do you prefer to find a job in your country?

Like most people, I prefer the help of the internet to find a job.

Q32. Is it easy to find a job in your country?

I would say that, with the increasing population and decreasing opportunities, it is getting harder by the day to find a suitable job in my country.

Q33. How do schools prepare students to get a job they like?

Schools prepare their students in various ways to get a job they have always aspired. For instance, they groom their personality or hold various seminars for them.

Q34. What improvements should schools have to identify student talent?

Schools should improve the way they hold co-curricular activities to tap into latent talent. They should encourage all students to participate in various activities so they can actually find out all the students' talents.

Q35. What do you think about public holidays?

Public holidays are the common celebrations on various occasions and are very important for the integrity of our society.

Q36. Do you think there are enough public holidays?

Yes, I think there are enough public holidays regarding different religions, cultures and festivals.

Q37. Do you like photographs?

Yes, I like photographs, because they refresh my memory and give me happiness.

Q38. Is photography a good profession in your country?

Yes, because the media cannot exist without photography. Moreover, photography is becoming a lucrative profession among youngsters, as it is commonly used in every field.

Q39. Explain the climate of your town.

The climate of my town is quite extreme. It is too hot in summer and too cold in the winters.

Q40. Discuss the type of food Indians like.

Indians, I think, like traditional food, and the taste differs from state to state.

Q41. Comment on the dressing sense of youngsters.

Youngsters almost everywhere in the world prefer trendy and branded clothes.

Q42. What types of animals are found in your locality?

I live in a posh locality so there are no animals that are found.

Q43. Would you like to change your name? Why?

Sorry, my name is my identity. Moreover, it was baptised and is a gift from my family.

Q44. What kind of gifts should be given to children?

Gifts that enhance their creativity, keep them busy and become a source of motivation for learning.

Q45. Do you like to have food with your family or alone?

I love having food with my family because it is a great bonding time. Moreover, food is enjoyed more when shared.

Q46. What should we do to keep ourselves busy?

We can keep ourselves busy by making optimum utilization of our hobbies.

Q47. What are the different sources of exercise?

Some different sources of exercise can be yoga, walking, running or dancing.

Q48. How can we get rid of stress?

We can get rid of our stress by indulging in our hobbies, like listening to music or sometimes even travelling.

Q49. How can music and exercise help us get rid of stress?

Since music and exercise are stress busters, they can immediately change our mood and divert our attention.

Q50. When do you listen to music?

I like to listen to music during my leisure time. It gives me relaxation and peace of mind.

Q51. Do you think you can be friends with only those people who have similar character as yours?

No, I don't think that I can only be friends with those who have similar characteristics as ours, because friendship is all about understanding.

Yes, I prefer my friends to some extent to be like-minded, because then it is easy to develop understanding and compatibility.

Q52. Do you think hobbies are a waste of time?

Sorry, no, because they play a significant role in mitigating unavoidable stress, as they provide us with an outlet for creativity and distraction and something to look forward to.

Q53. What are your strengths and weaknesses?

I believe my strength is that I am optimistic and dedicated person. My weakness is that I am short-tempered. But I'm working on it with anger control exercises.

Q54. What is adulteration?

The process of mixing impure substances into a pure product is known as adulteration.

Q55. How can we reduce it?

We can reduce it by implementing strict laws like cancelling the licenses of people who are involved in it.

Q56. Do you think people need a day off every week?

Yes, definitely. It is very important to de-stress. Moreover, they can complete any pending work.

Q57. What is more important for you, family or friends?

Both are very dear to me. But for me my family will always be my top priority because family, gives the sense of who you are and from where you come from. They are our blood and our heritage. Whereas, friends equally important as there are many secrets that one likes to entrusts with his/her friends only.

Q58. Do you prefer one long trip or many short trips?

I prefer short trips because it does not break the momentum of my work.

Q59. What is more important, money or family?

I believe both are important, because money gives me comfort while family gives me happiness.

Q60. Describe the turning point of your life.

The turning point of my life was when I decided to take the IELTS test. I became more organized, hard-working and dedicated to my work.

Q61. Describe the most memorable point of your life.

The most memorable point of my life was when I planned to migrate for a better future (getting a job, birthday or any other achievement).

Q62. Do men and women spend their leisure time in different ways?

Leisure activities are never gender-based, so it depends on the personal choice.

Q63. Who is your favourite relative? Why?

My favourite relative is my uncle, who is well-settled in Canada and is a very practical, optimistic and good decision-maker. He always guides me to choose the right path and be morally upright, which was valuable advice in choosing my career.

Q64. Which is better, single gender education or co-education?

In my opinion, co-education is better because it gives a sense of competition and discipline among students. Moreover, it also helps in understanding the potential of everyone, as it teaches that boys and girls can do the same things. It also increases the respect held for each other.

Q65. What are the reasons of the differences between parents and children?

The biggest difference occurs due to the generation gap. When both groups are not able to understand each other's point of view, it creates differences.

Q66. What is the role of extracurricular activities in schools and colleges?

Extracurricular activities teach discipline and cultural tolerance, and also help students to expand their network, which is beneficial for exploring career opportunities.

Q67. Which is the better option, staying in a hostel or staying at home while studying?

It is quite debatable, because both have their benefits. Staying in a hostel makes us self-dependent, confident and more organized. A house, on the other hand, gives us protection and comfort.

Q68. What do you have to say about Indian students migrating to foreign countries for higher studies?

I would say that, to explore more and better opportunities in their respective field and also to get an international exposure, Indian students are migrating abroad for higher studies. Moreover, developed countries promise quality education with international studies.

Q69. Which is the best method to teach very young children?

In my opinion, playing and teaching is the best method because it is very entertaining, which increases the child's retention.

Q70. Do you think that capital punishment (death sentence) is justified?

According to me, if the crime is of a heinous nature, capital punishment should be awarded to the accused, as it would act as a deterrent and will create a feeling of fear in the mind of the offenders.

Q71. How can music be used to teach very young children?

Teaching music to children can be very challenging. I am of the opinion that, if music is included as part of their curriculum, it would be easier to teach them.

Q72. What are the different types of water sports?

There are a variety of water sports like swimming, surfing, boating, white-water river rafting and fishing.

Q73. Do you think technology is necessary?

Yes, technology is necessary, as it makes our work fast, errorless, more organised and keeps us updated.

Q74. How often do you use technology?

I quite often technology use because it makes my work effortless, and it enables me to face international challenges.

Q75. Do you like dancing?

Yes, absolutely. It's a good exercise and gives me happiness.

Q76. Are there any music concerts held in your city?

Yes, music concerts are held in my city, because people enjoy attending them and seeing the celebrities who are a part of it.

Q77. Do you prefer a live concert or music on mobile phone?

I prefer music on my phone because I have a variety of options and can listen to music according to my mood. Moreover, there is no disturbance.

Q78. Who is your favourite singer?

There is a plethora of good singers these days but my favourite is... because his/her voice is very melodious.

Q79. Why do we need neighbours?

Neighbours provide security and can be instant help during an emergency. Some neighbours can be good companions.

Q80. How much freedom should be given to the teenagers?

Teenage is a growing age between 13 and 19. There are certain biological changes taking place that lead them to often be confused and emotional, ending up with them making rash decisions. Therefore, complete freedom can be disastrous, as this is the age when children can be easily misled by friends or the media.

Q81. How has the role of women changed in society?

The role of women has changed drastically in society. Nowadays, women are qualified and working, which is a family support.

Q82. Do you think Indian women are different from Western women?

Yes, Indian women are more attached to their culture and tradition, whereas Western women are mostly job-oriented and highly career-conscious.

Q83. Do you think that women alone should be responsible for bringing up the children?

Sorry (no), I feel it is the collective responsibility for children to be nurtured by the mother and father.

Q84. What is the difference between writing a letter and sending an email?

Letter-writing is a slow process and a hand-written document. It is an old mode of communication, whereas emails are messages sent through computers. Emails are very fast and have created a revolution in the field of communication.

Q85. Talk about someone who has made a great contribution in your society?

There are many business celebrities who have contributed to the economy of the country by generating jobs, reducing unemployment and increasing the economic standards of the people.

Q86. Tell me something about the education system in your country.

In my country, both traditional and online studies are popular. Students choose according to their understanding.

Q87. Now, we will talk about sleep. How many hours do you sleep in a day?

On an average, I sleep around 7–8 hours in a day, because it is clinically advised and keeps me healthy and active.

Q88. How many hours do you think people need to sleep?

I think different people have different sleeping patterns and requirements. But still, on average 8–9 hours should be enough.

Q89. What do you do when you feel sleepy but have to stay awake?

I do a variety of things to stay awake at that point, like I have a cup of tea or coffee, splash some water in my eyes or have an energy drink.

Q90. What are the positive and negative points of living in your hometown?

For the positive points, I would say my hometown has many facilities like transportation, education and medical services.

But for the negative ones, it's very crowded and polluted, since it's a developing city with many teething problems.

Q91. Discuss the health/education facilities in your area.

I live in a posh area with good schools and hospitals, so in my area the majority of people are healthy. Also, there are various coaching centres nearby, pertaining to various competitive fields that cater to fulfilling the educational needs of the students.

Q92. Do you want any change to be introduced to your area?

Yes, all I want are changes like broader roads, public parks and parking facilities.

Q93. How is the public transport in your area?

Luckily, the public transport in my area is very well-connected.

Q94. What is more important health or wealth?

I believe both are equally important, as one cannot be achieved without the other.

Q95. How does modern lifestyle lead to health-related issues?

A modern lifestyle results in high level of stress, which can lead to many diseases and disorders like hypertension and depression.

Q96. Who do you think lives more healthy life, a person living in city or village?

Although the health of a person depends on their lifestyle, one living in a village will usually have the upper hand, with a less hostile environment.

Q97. Is it advisable to go for a regular body check-up?

As we know that prevention is better than cure, regular check-ups help in detecting the disease at the very first stage.

Q98. How many hours do you think a person should work?

A person on an average should work only between 8–9 hours, depending on deadlines.

Q99. Let's talk about movies. Do you think films on real-life events or history should be made?

Yes, as it can give us deep knowledge about a period of time we are not familiar with.

Q100. Do you think we should ban movies showing violence?

Yes, as they can hamper the minds of children, who might learn negative things from it. Movies are the mirror of society, so they have a great impact on every section.

Q101. Let's talk about meditation. Do you prefer meditation?

Yes, sometimes. I do it because I find it very relaxing.

Q102. What is the future of meditation?

Since stress levels are at an all-time high these days, I think the future of meditation is very bright and popular.

Q103. What do people in your area do to get relaxation?

People in my area go for a regular walk or talk to each other in order to get relaxation. Like old people go for yoga or laughter exercises, while children play on swings and enjoy slides in the park near my house.

Q104. What are the effects of stress on people?

Stress has many negative effects on people, such as depression, anxiety, insomnia and negativity in life.

Q105. What are the various reasons for stress?

In my opinion, a lack of time management and an inability to set priorities cause stress because the workload nowadays is increasing and targets are unachievable.

Q106. In future, what type of activities do you think will be popular?

In future, according to me, indoor activities will be more popular because digitalization is at its peak.

Q107. What are the benefits of outdoor activities?

The benefits of outdoor activities are that they increase our stamina, give us a different environment and keep us physically fit.

Q108. What are a few outdoor activities?

Popular outdoor activities include playing cricket, football and going for a walk.

Q109. Define true friendship.

In my opinion, a true friendship has complete understanding and compatibility and is unconditional.

Q110. How do you manage disputes in your friendship?

I manage disputes in my friendship by resolving any misunderstanding through confrontation.

Q111. Do you take advice from people other than your family members?

Yes, sometimes I take advice from my teachers, friends and even my relatives. I like to take advice from people who have expertise with my situation.

Q112. Whose advice do youngsters follow more, friends or family members?

In my opinion, youngsters trust their friends blindly, rather than their family members, because they are their companions and understand them well.

Q113. Which advertisements according to you have better effect TV or newspapers and why?

I feel adverts on TV have a better effect because of its audio-visual impact on the people.

Q114. Should companies hire celebrities for advertisements? Why?

Yes, companies should hire celebrities for advertisements, since they are the role models and have public followings. These can profit the companies in the long run.

Q115. What were your hobbies in childhood days?

The favourite hobbies in my childhood days were playing outdoor activities with my friends and watching TV.

Q116. Are the hobbies of boys different from those of girls?

Hobbies are not based on the gender of a person; these activities depend on the interest of a particular person.

Q117. Do the hobbies distract the attention of children from studies?

I feel hobbies refresh the mind and even help to reduce the stress of study pressure. So no, they do not distract children from not studying.

Q118. Which is the best source of getting news, TV, the newspaper or radio? Why?

I think TV is the best source of getting news because of its fast-breaking news services and the audio-visual impact it has.

Q119. Will newspaper lose their importance in future?

Since the newspaper is one of the most important sources to get our news from, I don't believe it will vanish in the near future. It has a far and wide reach and is the traditional way of getting in touch with the world.

Q120. Can the internet replace the newspaper?

In my opinion, the internet cannot replace the newspaper in the near future, because it is still in its developing stages, whereas the newspaper is preferred by every traditional news-seeker.

Q121. What types of programs are popular in your country?

Programmes like daily soaps, comedy shows and reality talent search competitions are extremely popular.

Q122. How many hours in a day should a child watch television?

A child should not watch TV from more than 1–2 hours, since it can lead to eyesight problems.

Q123. Does watching television affect the behaviour of children?

Yes, children are still in the early stage of their life where they learn how to behave, so they try to imitate what they say and it can hamper with their behaviour.

Q124. What are the effects of television/radio on new generation?

The new generation, or gen X as we call it these days, stays updated and gets awareness from television and radio.

Q125. What should the government do to increase the popularity of radio?

The government should introduce new types of interesting shows that not only provide knowledge but also entertainment.

Q126. What type of programs should be broadcasted more on radio?

Programmes that not only entertain people but also increase their knowledge and make them aware about the world should be broadcasted more on the radio.

Q127. What are the advantages offered by radio over TV?

Radio is not only pocket-friendly but also a source of information.

Q128. What are the reasons behind noise pollution?

Various reasons such as loud speakers, DJ systems, pressure horns and construction sites are responsible for noise pollution.

Q129. What actions can be taken to reduce noise pollution?

We can, first of all, make some noise-free areas for the elderly and students. Then, we can create awareness among the masses and plant trees and other sound-absorbing material on the roadsides.

Q130. Can the police or local authorities take any action to reduce the noise pollution?

Yes, they can very well create strictness in the area by imposing a penalty on those who make excessive noise.

Q131. What actions can be taken against people who create noise?

They can be fined heavily and their source of noise can be confiscated.

Q132. What types of exercises can a person do in your city?

Exercises like walking, lifting weights and yoga can be easily done in my city.

Q133. What are the benefits of doing exercise?

Various benefits of exercising are that it keeps us fit and increases our stamina.

Q134. What types of exercises are becoming more popular nowadays?

Meditation, sports and dancing are popular exercises these days.

Q135. How do people of your society keep themselves fit?

People in my society can be found doing regular walk almost every day in the parks located in my town.

Q136. Do you think going to the gym has become a status symbol?

Yes, I feel that it has somewhat become a status symbol, especially among the youngsters, because these days it's not about staying fit but looking good.

Q137. Do you like to see paintings which are hanged on the wall in your house?

Oh yes, I love seeing paintings hung on the walls of my house, because those paintings are religious and I feel very calm and relaxed staring at them.

Q138. How does an artist get ideas on what to paint?

An artist, being creative, might get inspired by various things like a trip or a book, or maybe a movie.

Q139. What is the difference between painting and photography?

The technical difference between the two is that a painting is typically hand-made and can be imaginative, whereas a picture is taken digitally and is always real.

Q140. How many times a day you receive calls?

About 4–5 calls from my work and few from couple of friends.

Q141. What is the difference between mobile phones and landline phones?

Mobile phones, as we all know, are portable and can perform various functions, whereas a landline can only make calls and is stuck at one place.

Q142. Which is your favourite mode of communication?

I am a very traditional person, so my favourite mode of communication is face-to-face.

OR

Since I'm a very tech-savvy person, I prefer either chats through text or video calling through my phone.

Q143. Which forms of technology are you using at home or office?

I use the latest technology both in my office and at home. For instance, I use my laptop both at home and in the office, and I have an A.C installed in both places.

Q144. What are the good and bad effects of internet?

The internet is the fastest source of information and best source to keep us connected, whereas the vast use of the internet has given birth to many cyber-crimes.

Q145. What are the applications of a computer?

The computer has various applications, such as for calculations, the internet, making projects and presentations and gaining a technical understanding of a subject.

Q146. How are the computer helpful in education?

They help us make projects, give us quick information and can model a practical part of various subjects in schools and colleges,

Q147. Why do people get attracted to celebrities?

Since celebrities are role models and have a desirable lifestyle, people tend to follow them blindly and try to imitate them and their lifestyle.

Q148. Do you think endorsement by celebrities is the right option?

Yes, I think it is right, because it not only helps in product sales but also makes people aware about a new product in the market. But it is also the responsibility of the celebrities to choose the product carefully and communicate the right message to the public..

Q 149. What are its impacts on the new generation?

As we discussed before, the young generation follows celebrities blindly, so it can have both positive and negative impacts on them, depending on the kind of actions they take.

CUE
CARDS

Cue Cards

1. Gardening

1. Do you like gardening?

2. Should gardening be taught in school?

3. What is importance of plants?

It is a process to grow and nourish the plants and maintain the green belt, which reduces pollution. A garden can be in the house or in a locality. With the development of science and technology, gardening has become very technical, because there are new techniques, fertilizers and hybrid plants. It is an interesting subject which nowadays is becoming a part of environmental sciences. Among children, they can develop the interest if they are assigned the task. As it is a practical subject and the interest can be comfortably developed by watching the regular growth of plants. Nowadays the trend of organic vegetables has increased as they are free from any pesticides.

I have a small garden in my house. I watch the plants growing and changing their shapes. I don't have much technical awareness about gardening but I take care of the plants by watering them and see that they don't suffer from any type of diseases. I have a gardener who maintains our garden and also has created beautiful landscape in my garden. It is an elevated area which has a small waterfall, different sized plants and also some beautiful lights. Everyone admires my garden and it has also become my pride.

Discussion Questions:

- Are people in your society fond of gardening?

  _____

  _____

- Are there a lot of plants in your locality?

  _____

  _____

- How do plants help us in environmental problems?

  _____

  _____

- Do you think that gardening should be taught to a child from school days?

  _____

  _____

2. Success

1. What is success for you?

2. What is importance of success?

3. Talk about a successful moment of your life?

Success is a journey and not a destination. It is a state of mind which makes the person feels happy on his achievement. It may be because of hard work or by luck. A successful person is always a respectable person. Success can be in different fields: academic, financial or career. Success provides confidence, security, a sense of well-being, the ability to concentrate at a greater level, hope and leadership. It drives us forward, it is something we all seek, something which we if fail to achieve, can be quite devasting. Hence, success is incredibly important to each one of us.

I am a successful person because I always work on my flaws. There are a lot of instances when I achieved success; in school, college and even competitions. It has made me confident and optimistic person.

I believe my most successful moment is when I got accepted onto a study programme in Delhi University. I am naturally quite a shy person so being thousands of miles away from friends and family was daunting. It was a life time opportunity for which I worked very hard. It gave me a chance to participate in so many activities which otherwise I would have never taken part in before.

Even today these experience till impacts my life. I am much more confident than before. This one experience in my life has encouraged and motivated me to more likely try new things of which I am initially afraid of. I would from my personal experience strongly recommend that students should participate in such study programmes if they have the opportunity. I learned so much and gained many experiences which have helped me in my academics and even in my life.

Discussion Questions

- Is being successful only being rich?

  _____

  _____

- What is the difference between being rich and being successful?

  _____

  _____

- Do you think that the behaviour of a person changes with the success level?

  _____

  _____

- In the future, if you will be successful, what type of things will you do for the betterment of society?

  _____

  _____

3. Painting

1. What is painting?
2. Should painting be included as a compulsory subject in education?
3. What type of paintings do you like?

Painting is a creative art. It is a natural talent, a very good hobby and a profession. Painting is an important form in the visual arts, bringing in elements such as drawing, gesture or abstraction. There are various types of paintings like figure paintings, modern art, landscape paintings, portrait paintings etc. I personally like landscape and portrait paintings. Landscape painting is a kind of a painting that covers a depiction of natural scenery such as trees, mountains, valleys, rivers and forests. What I have personally noticed in such kind of paintings is that sky is always included in the view, and weather is often an element of composition. On the other hand portrait painting are representations of a person, in which the face and expressions is predominant. The intent of the painter is to display the personality and even the mood of the person. Discussing further it is undoubtedly true that nowadays a proper curriculum planning has become a vital part of education. Many people feel that it is important for the students to be taught painting in schools as compulsory subject. Painting helps to enhance the creativity in children. This in turn helps them to build their imagination and can also broaden their horizon or way of thinking. Also, being engaged in such activity helps students to relax by breaking the monotonous job of studying academics.

On the other hand, there are certain circumstances wherein the idea of including painting in curriculum is not welcomed by the students and even their parents. For instance, a child who is more interested in playing sports will feel that it is a waste of time. Instead it would be more rewarding if he invests his time in practising sports. Hence I feel that it will not be a good idea to include painting as a part of curriculum as it would unnecessary put pressure on the students who are good in other fields.

Discussion Questions

- Do you think that painting divert the attention of students from their studies?

  _____

  _____

- Can painting be turned into a good profession?

  _____

  _____

- Can you do any special type of painting?

  _____

  _____

- Can you tell what the difference is between a painting and a photograph?

  _____

  _____

- Have you heard about any famous painter of your country? If yes can you tell about that painter?

  _____

  _____

- Do you admire painting?

  _____

  _____

4. Statue

1. What is a statue?

2. What is the importance of statues?/Why are they made?

3. Is there any eye-catching statue near your area?

A statue is a piece of art that reflects the culture and tradition of any famous personality. It is a free-standing sculpture in which the realistic, full length figures of persons or animals or non-representational forms are carved in a durable material like wood, metal, or stone. Every statue generally has its historical background which becomes a source of learning. Many statutes are placed in a public places as public art. Statues are made of historical, social or political personalities. For instance statute of Sardar Vallabhai Patel who was the first Home minister of independent India is located in the state of Gujrat, India. This statue is also known as statue of unity and is the world's tallest statute with a height of 182 meters. The statute of unity surely deserves a place in the history of the world. Nit joins an impressive list of manmade structures that have earned admiration of the world through generations. Statues reflect the traditional and historical background of the city. There is a very famous statute in my area which is of Maharaja Ranjit Singh. Itis very well-maintained statue of Amritsar. It depicts about the rich culture of Punjab. Maharaja Ranjit Singh legacy includes a period of Sikh culture and artistic renaissance, including the rebuilding of Harimandar sahib in Amritsar as well as other major gurudwaras. These are just few of the examples that I have discussed. To conclude, I would like to say that statues are the centre of attraction for the tourists and government should spread awareness by conducting a sustained worldwide campaign to inform and educate about the new marvels. Even a substantial internal marketing effort can be used to promote awareness and to attract the tourists.

Discussion Questions

• Do you think that government should **provide** money to build statue?

_____

_____

• Is statue an attraction for tourists?

_____

_____

- What is your opinion about statues?

  _____

  _____

- Do you think that statues are necessary to increase the beauty of a nation?

  _____

  _____

- Do you admire any statue? If yes tell me about that statue?

  _____

  _____

5. Workplace

1. What is a workplace?

2. What is the importance of workplace?

3. What should be the working hours?

4. Do colleagues play a vital role in making suitable environment at a workplace?

5. What kind of relations do you have with your colleagues?

It is a premise where we put our maximum efforts to get good rewards. The productivity of the work depends on the atmosphere of the workplace. The working condition should be very healthy and professional. Strong work ethics and values play an important role in the workplace. The behaviour of the employees promotes a good and a cooperating environment in an organization. If the behaviour of the employees is not good it creates a hostile environment which hampers the overall results and makes it difficult to achieve the set targets. Perhaps it is essential that the employees adhere to the good behaviour in an organization and to follow the rules and the code of conduct within the workplace. Another important issue to be discussed is the working hours in an organization. I believe that it is very essential to have a flexible working hours so that it does not puts a lot of pressure on the employees. In case of emergency or any other contingency the organizations should be considerate in permitting leaves if necessary. Apart from this working hours may vary according to the work load. Now further, I would like to discuss my experience at my workplace. I am currently working in an

MNC based in............(eg Gurgaon). It is a US based company and the work culture at my organization is very cordial. Regardless of the fact how much this organization has helped me to groom my overall personality I also share a very good relationship with my fellow colleagues. I personally believe that workplace relationships directly affect a worker's ability and drives a person to succeed.

Discussion questions

- What are the essential facilities required by an employee in a workplace?

  _____

  _____

- Say something about the role of the workplace in job satisfaction.

  _____

  _____

- Do workplaces have some impact on the market image of a company?

  _____

  _____

- Have you ever had a job? How was your workplace?

  _____

  _____

- What changes have you experienced in the workplace of the present day as compared to the past generations workplace?

  _____

  _____

6. Friendship

1. What is friendship according you?
2. Are friends important in your life?
3. To what extend would you go for your friends?
4. What is more important – friends or family?
5. Share an incident of your friendship.

Friendship is an unconditional relationship between two or more than two people. Categorically speaking, friendship is of two types: long term and short term. It is without any personal motive, whereas a professional friendship is with a purpose. It is as important as to have friends as it is to have a family. Good friends help, guide and support us at every stage. Friends give us emotional support, they help us during difficult times and make us feel special. Friends are extremely important to everyone. They form an essential part of our lives. Life becomes more enjoyable and bearable when we have good friends around. They help in bringing out the best in each other by extending help when it comes to studies and other activities. I am an extroverted person. I have a number of friends. But ABC is my bosom-buddy. She is an optimistic person and whenever I am down emotionally, I turn to my best friend. She knows how to calm me and support me at such a time. Whenever I need any guidance regarding handling my relationships, managing my studies or participating in any other activities she is always there to guide me. I remember when we were assigned a project on blind institute, we assisted each other in completing the project. I remember she was unable to finish her project due to a high fever, so I helped her and she got a good assessment. There are many incidents when we both extended our help to each other. Besides this, our families are also on friendly terms. It is believed that friendship is no doubt a blessing, but there are many reasons for ending friendships. No doubt we are very thick friends, but sometimes we argue over trifle matters. There are dissimilarities between us. I am very calm and she sometimes gets aggressive on petty issues. But we always resolve our matters by confronting each other.

Discussion Questions

- Is friendship important in your culture? How many close friends do you have?

  _____

  _____

- Are friends more important than family?

  _____

  _____

- What are important things among good friends?

  _____

  _____

- Do you have any friends from a foreign country?

  _____

  _____

- What are the differences between real life and pen friends?

  _____

  _____

7. River

1. Importance of river.

2. Have you ever been to a river?

3. Connection of river with religion.

4. Are there any drawbacks of living near a river?

5. Talk about a river or a lake you visited?

The river is a natural source of water. It is the biggest gift of God that benefits living beings. Rivers carry water and nutrients to areas all around the earth. They play a very important role in the water cycle, acting as drainage channels for surface water. Rivers provide excellent habitat and food for many of earth's organisms. They provide us with fresh water which is helpful for various purposes such as drinking, cleaning, washing etc. Importance of rivers cannot be stated in just few words. There are various civilizations formed around rivers. Even in today's date many villages and cities are based near rivers. They are not only important to human beings but also serve a great purpose to the animals and trees as well. There are various aquatic animals which breed in rivers. They form a part of ecosystem which is very important to maintain the balance in the food chain. Regardless of the advantages of river it also shares a close nexus with religion. The rivers in Indian culture holds sacred significance. Alaknanda, Ganga, Narmada etc. are some of the rivers that holds religious importance. It is believed that the water of these rivers not only purifies objects for ritual use, but can make a person clean, externally as well as spiritually. The significance of different rivers manifests differently in different religions and beliefs. It is not surprising that everything comes with its own disadvantages and the river with all its benefits also has its downside. Areas like this are always prone to some infections from various insects that breeds on or around water logged areas such as mosquitos which are the chief source of malaria and dengue. Another major disadvantage is that flooding is a regular thing in the riverine area and can pose a lot of negative effects on people that live close to the river bank. I would like to talk about a lake where I visited several times with my family and my friends. It is a Sukhna lake in Chandigarh. It is situated at the foothills of Shivalik hills. It is an important part of Chandigarh which adds to its beauty. People can also enjoy boating in that lake. There was also an arrangement for breakfast, lunch and dinner. A number of shops are situated on the edge of the lake. I enjoyed a cup of coffee. It was a beautiful experience as it a pollution free area and one get relief from stressful life by visiting there.

Discussion Questions

- What are the differences between a road trip and a boat trip?

  _____

  _____

- What is the importance of the river in your country?

  _____

  _____

- How was your experience of visiting the river?

  _____

  _____

- Do you think that a trip to the river should be organized in schools?

  _____

  _____

8. Shop

1. Describe a shop.
2. What changes have you seen in present shops?
3. Do you think big shops are eating the small shops?
4. Which is your favourite shopping outlet?

A shop is an outlet from where various products can be purchased through plastic currency. Earlier most of the shopping was done in traditional shops like purchasing from local butchers, bakers, Grocers etc. Over the years as supermarkets are trending the concept of shopping has drastically changed. As these supermarkets cater the needs of the customers by providing them with variety of articles under one roof, the small corner shops have disappeared. The growth of supermarkets has been the success story over the period of time and this has certainly affected the small corner shops. As I am from Amritsar my favourite shopping outlet is Trillium mall. It is situated in heart of the city. The area is easily accessible. It is a huge mall with two wings which offers a great shopping experience including variety of restaurants, cafes, lounges, various clothing stores and also cinema theatre. The trillium shopping mall hosts many renowned brands and offers distinctive shopping experience. The food court is something that I love about this shopping mall. With the safest environment, this is an ideal shopping centre for all types of shoppers. I visit this shopping mall because almost everything is available under one roof which makes it quite convenient. I like this shopping mall mostly because of the quality products and good prices they offer. Apart from that the security customer service and nice environment also attracts me to shop from this mall. Another reason that affects my shopping decision from this shopping mall is its distance from my house. It takes only 10 minutes to reach there and these are quite few of the reasons I decide to shop here.

Discussion Questions

- How do village shops differ from cities?

  _____

  _____

- What basic facilities do you think a shop should provide?

  _____

  _____

- Describe a bad/good experience you had while shopping?

  _____

  _____

- What changes do you experience in your shopping routine with the development of the internet?

_____

_____

9. Zoo/Educational Visit

1. What is a zoo?

2. Compare zoos of developing countries with developed countries?.

3. What do you learn after visiting a zoo?

4. Should zoo be used as a source of entertainment?

A zoo is an open area where animals are kept under natural environment. Their health, comfort and safety are properly taken care of. It provides/ and also serves as a very good way of practical education where we can observe the behaviour of different species of animals very closely. Scientist and students both benefit out of it. A visit to a zoo is always very interesting. It adds to our knowledge. As the area of the zoo is very big, like the natural habitats for the animals, they adjust to this environment and learn eventually how to survive there. Mostly there is always an entry ticket to the zoo which helps to raise the funds for maintenance of the zoo.

I remember my visit to Chatbir zoo in Chandigarh. It is very well maintained and is the biggest attraction for the tourists. The zoo is divided into different sections. First of all, I saw a pond in which there were many water birds like ducks and cranes. One the other side was the monkey section. It was quite interesting to watch them. Later, I saw the section in which other wild animals like lions, tigers, leopards were kept in huge cages. The tiger was very majestic. Another section was the birds section. Beautiful birds from all over the world were there in cages. They were chirping. There were white parrots which was new to me. There was another section which was totally separate and that was the section of reptiles in which numerous snakes and lizards from all over the world were kept. The habitat, food habits, species etc. of each and every animal was written in front of the cages. I gained a lot of knowledge about the animals. I was impressed by the discipline maintained in the zoo. There were many security guards to check behaviour of the visitors. There were even signboards which warned the visitors not to tease the animals. Even the loud music was not allowed. Overall my visit to the zoo was very knowledgeable and fun.

Discussion Questions

- Is it good to lock animals in cages?

  _____

  _____

- What do you think about experimentation on animals?

  _____

  _____

- Which is better to you, zoos or wildlife sanctuaries?

  _____

  _____

- What is the role of the government to increase the popularity of zoos?

  _____

  _____

- Do you think that zoos can also be a tourist attraction?

  _____

  _____

10. Child

1. Who is a child?

   Beautiful creation of nature.

2. Have you met any small child?

   My niece

3. How much would you like to spend with them?

   Not much because I am busy.

4. How do you feel when you play with a small child?

   Relaxed and distressed

5. Why?

   Because she is very innocent and is away from day to day serious problems.

6. What do you learn from young child?

   Honesty and innocence

7. Should all the questions of a young child be answered?

   Yes, because their understanding does not match ours. It should be according to their mental level.

8. Do you feel irritated sometimes?

   I have patience and I always keep my cool.

9. Qualities of a good story teller?

   Binding factor

10. Have you ever narrated a story to a child?

    Yes, fantasies, imagination and fairy tales.

11. Do you remember any?

    No sir, I read it from the book.

12. Why do old people/grandparents enjoy child's company?

    Because they are cute, innocent and inquisitive.

13. Difference between past and present?

    Past-children were not technically sound. But in this hi-tech world even they are interested in technology.

Discussion Questions

- Why is it hard for parents to raise a child?

  _____

  _____

- What things can children learn from toys?

  _____

  _____

- What do you think about children from rich families who have lots of toys?

  _____

  _____

- How do you think children and teenagers are different?

  _____

  _____

- Do you think children today are happier than children in the past?

  _____

  _____

11. Pollution

1. Water pollution

   Contamination of water

   Not fit for consumption

   Dump of industrial waste

   Leakage of oil from ships

   Poor sewage conditions

2. Air pollution

   Vehicles industry, burning of paddy, crackers

3. Soil pollution

   Deforestation: Removal of upper soil layer, bare land, lack of crop rotation

4. Thermal pollution

   Unnecessary climatic changes, global warming, nuclear testing

5. Noise pollution

   Hampers hearing capacity

Discussion Question

- How can we tackle the increasing problem of pollution?

- What types of activities are giving birth to various types of pollution?

- What problems do mankind face by such pollution?

- Do you think that be the implementation of law the problem of pollution can be solved?

12. Bank Account

1. Do you have a bank account?
2. In which bank do you have an account?
3. What interest rate do they charge?
4. What are the benefits of opening a bank account?
5. What other type of facilities they provide?

The word 'bank' means trust. It is building a relationship between customers and employees. A bank account is a way to transact money. It keeps money very safe and sometimes multiplies it according to the deposit. It is an organization that is completely regulated under the law. In the past, most of the banks were government-controlled banks. But due to globalization, private banking has become very popular in which the customers are provided with various other facilities and privileges. A bank account can be a deposit account, a credit card account, or any other type of account offered by a financial institution, and represents the funds that a customer has entrusted to the financial institution and from where the customers can make withdrawals. Regardless, bank account is only meant for bona fide citizens without any criminal record. The account can be of the native citizen or an NRI. There are various benefits of opening a bank account. They are safe and our money is protected from theft and money is federally insured. Apart from this they offer convenience. If we get an ATM or a debit card, we can withdraw money easily and can make payments at stores. Regardless of the fact, having a bank account is the easiest way to save money. Many of the banks offer an interest rate when we deposit our money in a savings account. The interest helps our money to grow over the time. Majority of the banks provide interest on savings account at 4% only. Few banks may also provide high interest rate at around 5–6%. This is the first and foremost criteria that we consider while looking for a bank account. We prefer opening a saving bank account with a bank that offers higher interest rates.

I have my bank account with ICCI bank. I have been a credible customer with this bank since 10 years. I have always been satisfied with their services. The best part of having a bank account with ICCI is that they offer spectrum of financial services for personal and corporate banking. It also offers services such as internet banking, ATM services, depository, financial advisory services and NRI services.

Discussion Questions

- Is it safe to have a bank account?

  _____

  _____

- Have you ever had a bad experience of visiting bank?

  _____

  _____

- Which is a better government bank or private banks?

  _____

  _____

- Do you use an internet banking facility?

  _____

  _____

13. Magazines

1. What is the importance of magazines?

2. Which magazine do you read?

3. What is the impact of magazines on youth?

4. What do you prefer – newspaper or magazine?

5. Are magazines informative or only entertaining?

A magazine is no doubt a form of print media that caters to almost every section of the society. They are source of entertainment and are also informational. Whether it's celebrity gossip, politics, or other topics, there is a wide range to choose from that will satisfy the reader's interest. Children, teenagers and even old people are able to find magazines of their liking. Magazines have been important to the world of publishing for many years and have brought enjoyment and entertainment to many people. They come in many genres like consumer magazines, business magazines, sports magazines, fashion magazines etc. The magazines also have great impact on youth. Most teen magazines focus in fashion, grooming and music idols. Articles about healthy eating, exercise, relationships, etc. guide teens through their life struggles. Features on academics and careers, motivate and encourage the youth in their endeavours. I personally prefer reading magazine rather than reading newspaper. I am of the opinion that magazines tend to enjoy high credibility because of the nature of its content and in addition to this magazines are typically read by highly interested audience because there are specific magazines for various topics. Perhaps of having my bent towards reading newspaper more I like to read political magazines during my leisure time and whenever I am travelling. It is a source of information and entertainment because the issues are latest and the language is very crisp. My favourite magazine is India Today which handles the latest burning issues. Sometimes, it deals with political affairs and even global issues. It is famous for its authentic information. This magazine has developed my group discussion skills and has also helped me in my assignments because the information is in detail and the data is very easy to understand. I like reading it in English because it helps me develop my communication skills.

Discussion Question

- What do you think are the important qualities for a news reporter?

  _____

  _____

- What's the main difference between newspaper and magazine?

  _____

  _____

- What's the function of report to society?

  _____

  _____

- What kind of books/newspapers/magazines do adolescents read in you society?

  _____

  _____

- With the popularity of internet, do you think newspapers and magazines will disappear?

  _____

  _____

14. Radio

1. Importance of radio?

2. Do you prefer listening to the radio?

3. Do you think that with the increasing technology, its popularity is decreasing?

4. What do elders think about radio?

Radio was the biggest invention of technology that became a mode of entertainment and information. We get news and music from different countries of the world through it, sitting in our own house. Nowadays, radios are run by batteries rather than electricity. They are small in size and are hence potable and can be easily taken from one place to another. There are many radio stations on a radio. They are of great use to us from hearing news to providing entertainment. It is also of great benefit to the traders as they come to know of the latest prices of different varieties of things. There are programmes on air that are full of information. . With the development of technology, radio stations became very compact and were almost in every city. As I am working, listening to radio is very easy, comfortable and entertaining for me. I can listen to it even on my mobile phone or while driving. As it is source of light entertainment, I like non-stop music channel in which there are a variety of songs in Hindi, Punjabi and English. Moreover, the announcer of the programme has melodious voice. I listen whenever I am free. The clarity of the programme is very good.

And I certainly think that with increasing technology the popularity of the radio is diminishing. To survive, radio must innovate, learn from other sources of media and take control of its path to maintain its unique position with advertisers and audiences. With the inevitable decline, radio needs to invest in strong and compelling digital services. Elders usually enjoy radio as they can connect themselves with it. Apart from this it is a great source of entertainment and information. People who have busy routine can listen to the songs or news and even important advertisements on radio in their cars or while they are travelling.

Discussion Questions

- Do you think that, with the development in technology, the trend of radio is diminishing?

  _____

  _____

- What can be done to increase the popularity of the radio?

  _____

  _____

- What type of attitude do youngsters have towards the radio?

  _____

  _____

- Why should the radio be preferred over television?

  _____

  _____

15. Advertisement

1. Do you like to watch adverts?

2. Does it affect the sales of the products?

3. Is it a correct source of spreading awareness?

4. Should companies hire celebrities for advertisements?

5. Is endorsement by celebrities a right thing?

Advertising is a process to enhance the sales of the product. It is the prime motive of any company to promote the product by informing the customer it's price and features. Companies use different methods to introduce the product. It can be print media i.e. newspapers and magazines and another can be e-media like TV and the internet. Certainly I like to watch adverts, as it updates me regarding the latest and even the existing trends in the markets. Advertising plays a very important role in customer's life. Customers are the people who buy the product only after they are made aware of the products available in the market. One of the main benefits that the companies reap through advertisements is that the companies which are in their introduction stage get a platform to launch the product. They often use flashy and attractive ads to make customers take a look on the products and purchase them. Certainly I am of the opinion that, advertisement helps to increase the sales of the product and plays a vital role for both the producer and the seller, as it helps the companies to know their competitors and plan accordingly to meet up the level of competition. Now discussing further about advertisement, these days many mainstream or A list celebrities endorse the products to advertise it. Celebrity endorsement or celebrity branding is literally a form of advertising where celebrities use their fame to promote the products. I believe that there is no harm if the products are endorsed by the celebrities. One of the main reasons is that people like to see a familiar face on a product and moreover it catches the viewers attention. It is a sure thing that when a product is endorsed by a celebrity it gets more recognition. A product if advertised by a celebrity has more effect on consumer than when it is advertised by a common person. For instance, when a health drink is endorsed by a sportsman, people believe it more than when the same is advertised by a common man. So endorsement of product by celebrities is very effective.

Discussion Questions

- What is the impact of advertisements on children?

  _____

  _____

- Have you ever purchased a product because of watching advertisement?

  _____

  _____

- Do advertisements provide reliable information or not?

  _____

  _____

- Which is the better way to advertise: audio-visual media or print media?

  _____

  _____

16. Dance

1. Do you like dancing?
2. Is it a good source of exercise?
3. What is the future of dancing?
4. Can you name your favourite dancer/choreographer?

Dancing is a whole-body workout that's actually fun. It is performing of an art form consisting of purposefully selected sequences of human movement. Dance can be categorized and described by its choreography, or by it historical period or place of origin. I am personally very fond of dancing. It is my hobby. These days many people irrespective of their age do dancing. The reason behind I developed interest in dancing is because of my friend who is an amazing dancer. She has been a great source of inspiration and motivated me to take dance as hobby. Apart from enjoying dancing as a hobby I truly believe that dancing is a great form of work out and is a good source of exercise. For instance, freestyle dancing which learnt recently offers an excellent type of aerobic exercise, it makes the heart pump faster and works on our muscles. It also assists in burning calories significantly faster. Hence, dancing has quite a few advantages. Discussing its further, the future of dancing is very bright. Dancing is a well-known talent or skill which would always be appreciated. Professional dancers or choreographers are the most talented people and their future is very wide. Working for big dancing companies will not only make them famous but also is a good paying profession. Moreover the demand of leaning flawless dance will always be there. As from time immemorial, dance has always been part of Indian celebration. Be it weddings or award ceremonies, the event cannot be completed without the shaking of a leg. Dancing will always remain and intrinsic part of our Indian culture. Explaining further, well, all dancers are mind blowing and perfect in their own forms. My personal favourite dancer or I should say choreographer is Pandit Birju Maharaj. He is a professional Khatak dancer. He can express dance only with hos facial expressions. I am trained in Khatak for 4 years. The way he does his each and every step is remarkable. I was personally trained by him and the way he teaches cannot be expressed in words. Well, this is the reason why he is my favourite dancer.

Discussion Questions

- Do you think that dancing can be taken up as a good profession?

- Have you ever learned any dance form?

- What kind of dancing do people in your city like?

- Is there any difference between traditional dancing and modern dancing?

- Do you think that people can dance only on special occasions?

17. Festival

1. What is a festival?

2. Why are they important?

3. Which is your favourite festival?

Festivals are the celebrations which revive the culture and tradition of the society. They are very important because they increase the feeling of brotherhood and interaction among the people. Almost all the festivals are rooted in cultures and traditions. They have mythological stories and strong meanings behind every festival. In the past people were more religious minded and they celebrated festivals in ethical manner. But due to global culture, and heterogeneous society, the intermixing of culture has increased. There are many festivals which people celebrate even without being attached to them. The common festivals are Christmas and Diwali.

Since I live in Punjab, where the culture is homogenous and the main occupation of people is agriculture, Baisakhi is a very common festival which people celebrate together with enthusiasm and zeal. For the Sikh community, Baisakhi has tremendous religious significance. As it was on a Baisakhi day, that Guru Gobind Singh ji, the tenth Sikh Guru laid the foundation of Panth Khalsa. This auspicious festival is celebrated all over India under different names and different sets of rituals and celebrations. Indeed the people of Punjab celebrate the festival of Baisakhi with exuberance and devotion. As the festival has tremendous importance in Sikh religion, major activities of the day are organized in Gurudwaras. People wake up early to prepare for the day. Many of them also take bath in the holy river to mark the auspicious occasion. After getting ready people pay visit to their neighbourhood Gurudwara and take part in the special prayer meeting organized for the day. At the end of the Baisakhi ardas, congregates receive specially prepared Kara Prasad. This is followed by guru ka langar or community lunch. Apart from the celebrations by the people this festival has a great significance for the farmers. For the farmers in Punjab and Haryana it marks for the new years time as it is the time to harvest the rabi crop. On Baishakhi, the famers thank god for the bountiful crop and pyar for good times ahead. People buy new clothes and make merry by singing, dancing and enjoying the best of the festive food. In several villages of Punjab Baishakhi fairs are organized where various recreational activities are there.

Discussion Questions

- Do you think that festivals nowadays have lost their original meaning?

  _____

  _____

- Is the celebration of festivals becoming modernized?

  _____

  _____

- What type of special food is associated with festivals in your country?

  _____

  _____

- Do you think we should celebrate every festival to understand others' cultures?

  _____

  _____

- How have celebrations changed with time?

  _____

  _____

18. Homework

1. What is the importance of homework?
2. Should it only be academic?
3. Do you think it is helpful or is it only a burden?

Homework is a revisional task assigned to a candidate for better performance. It keeps the candidate occupied and in touch with the studies. It is a part of traditional education and important method to make the candidate independent in his studies. It can be theoretical or practical. It depends on the subject.

Homework is sometimes a burden to teachers and students but still it is necessary. Some people doubt homework's effectiveness, but teachers and researchers agree homework is essential. Homework helps students get better grades in school. Homework is defined as basically defined as a class activity assigned to students as an extension or elaboration of a classroom work. Parents, students and teachers all sometimes wonder how useful homework is. Through studies examining the importance of homework many teachers and researchers hold an opinion that homework helps students achieve higher grades in school. Schools that assigned homework frequently showed higher student achievement than schools that assigned little homework. Studies have discovered that if teachers carefully plan homework, homework can be quite helpful. Homework has proven its effectiveness and is very powerful factor in students performance. Students should spend enough time on homework so that the subject is reinforced and their understanding to the topic discussed in class is revised and the conceptual understanding is improved.

Discussion Questions

- What type of homework do you think is healthy for the children?

  _____

  _____

- What are the reasons why children feel the burden of homework?

  _____

  _____

- Some people believe it is a good source to increase the knowledge of a child. What do you think?

  _____

  _____

- What type of homework would you get in your school days?

  _____

  _____

Are you in favour of homework or not?

Spider Charts

1. Time

➤ Use this spider chart to elaborate on the ideas as you go along the chart in the given time to cover all the necessary details which you might miss otherwise.

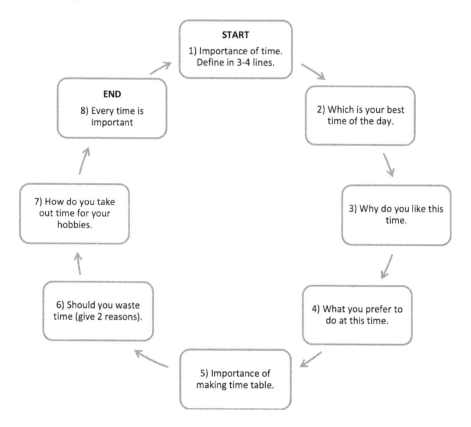

➤ Try it yourself and compare your answers with that at the back.

2. Teacher

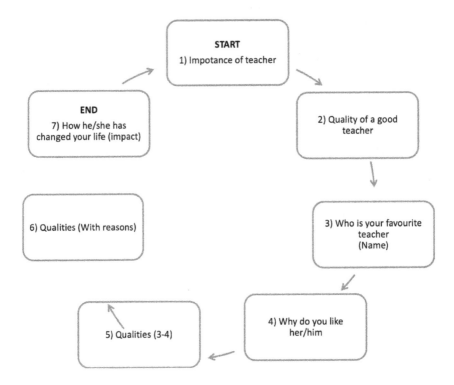

> Use this spider chart to make a cue card of 1–2 minutes and use all the points in serial order.

> Try and compare your answer with the solution.

SOLUTIONS

TIME

Time is the key to success and it waits for no one. It is very valuable because it never comes back. So, it is very important to value time and I never waste my time. No doubt, I'm an early riser and I feel very fresh in the morning. I am full of energy and I like to do my studies and meditation during morning. But my mornings are very hectic. I have to go for my classes so, I don't have enough time to enjoy my breakfast with my family or even read the newspaper. So, my favourite time is evening when I'm distressed from my work. This is the relaxing time when I enjoy going to gym, doing some workout and meeting friends. It is family time when we all members sit together, have dinner and I also watch TV. This is very relaxing. Sometimes, when the weather is pleasant, I like to go for an evening walk in the park opposite to my house. I am an organised person and believe in time management, which I do by making a time-table and following it sincerely. This increases my working capacity and motivates me to achieve my goals and targets, so I always respect every time of the day, and I'm very punctual.

TEACHER

A teacher is a friend, philosopher and a guide. I respect all my teachers and some of my teachers are my role model from my school days. I admire my communication teacher. She is highly motivating, optimistic and has complete knowledge about the subject matter. I like her teaching style and problem-solving techniques. No doubt, I have good understanding in English but I face problem of hesitation in public speaking. I used to feel demotivated. As I am planning to study abroad so this was a big inherence. I attended her classes regularly. I learnt many new words to express myself and she encourages me to participate in group discussions, debates and public speaking. This develops my confidence and it was a big chance. Now I am applying for the different interviews and foreign studies. She has helped me acquire knowledge on and an adequate hold over the subject. I will always be obliged for her time and consideration. She is very friendly and disciplined. All the students are regular and sincere in her lectures. In my opinion teacher plays a very important role in developing the interest of student.

JOB

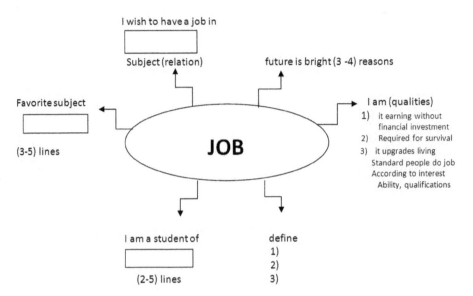

I wish to have a job in

Subject (relation)

future is bright (3 -4) reasons

Favorite subject

(3-5) lines

JOB

I am (qualities)
1) it earning without financial investment
2) Required for survival
3) it upgrades living Standard people do job According to interest Ability, qualifications

I am a student of

(2-5) lines

define
1)
2)
3)

SMART PHONES

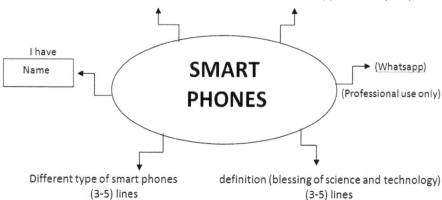

Features different applications in your phone

different application in your phone

I have
Name

SMART PHONES

(Whatsapp)
(Professional use only)

Different type of smart phones
(3-5) lines

definition (blessing of science and technology)
(3-5) lines

Clubbing of Cards

FAULTY PRODUCT

I am a **planned shopper.** I always buy the product after a complete survey because I **dislike wasting money.** I remember a **bad experience** of shopping. I was watching an **advertisement** it was about a mobile phone. I was very happy because the price was affordable and features were very good. I wanted to buy this cell phone from my **pocket money,** and I was planning to **gift** it to my mom. I went to the store, for the demo and bought the phone. I was very happy but very **shortly I was disappointed** because the product was faulty. The display was dim, keys were hard and quality of the sound was very poor. I became **sad** because I could not gift the phone to my mom. I went to the store and **lodged a complaint.** The salesman was very polite. He **apologized** and promised to deliver the new set within 15 days. I was happy when I got a new set but I learnt a **lesson** never to **buy the product in haste.** It was **a bad experience of shopping which eventually turned out to be a good one.**

QUESTIONS

1. Planned shopper
2. Dislike
3. Bad experience
4. Advertisement
5. Gift
6. Shortly disappointed
7. Sad moment
8. Lodged complaint
9. Apologize

10. Lesson

11. Bad experience which turned into good one

12. Buy in haste

13. Pocket money

14. Happy moment

Planned Shopper

1. Talk about your experience of shopping?

2. Do you prefer to shop after planning or not?

3. Which product you shopped and what was the experience?

   A. Talk about a product you purchased and disliked.

      1. What was it?

      2. From where did you buy?

      3. Why did you dislike it?

   B. Talk about bad experience of shopping

      1. What did you buy?

      2. Why the experience was bad?

      3. Which shopping is more safe (online or offline)?

   C. Talk about an advertisement you saw

      1. What was it about?

      2. What did you buy?

      3. How was the experience?

   D. Talk about a gift you wanted to give someone.

      1. What was it?

      2. Why you wanted to gift?

      3. To whom you wanted to gift?

4. What was the occasion?

5. How was your experience?

E. Talk about an occasion when you were disappointed?

1. What was it?

2. Why you were disappointed?

3. What did you miss?

F. Talk about a sad moment of your life

1. What was it?

2. Why do you think it was sad?

3. What did you miss?

4. What was your reaction?

G. Talk about a moment when you were angry and you have to lodged a complaint.

1. What was it?

2. Why it was important?

3. How did you manage?

H. Talk about an occasion when somebody apologized for his mistake.

1. What was it?

2. When was it?

3. How did you react?

4. Is it good to forgive?

I. Talk about a lesson you learnt from shopping.

1. What was it?

2. Why do you think it was important?

3. Would you repeat the mistake?

J. Talk about an occasion when a bad experience was turned into good happy moment

   1. What was it?

   2. Why do you think it was bad?

   3. How did it become good?

K. Talk about a decision you made in haste.

   1. What was it?

   2. What effect it had?

   3. What lesson did you learn?

L. What is the importance of pocket money?

   1. Do you receive pocket money?

   2. Talk about a product you bought from your pocket money?

   3. What was it?

   4. How did you feel?

   5. Share the experience?

F. Talk about a happy moment in your life.

   1. What was it?

   2. Why do you think you were happy?

   3. Was it real happiness or not?

<u>Note:</u> All the underlined words are cue cards. You can study and build the ideas to make the cue cards by yourself.

WALK

Describe a Walk That You Enjoyed.

- When was it?

- Where was it?

- With whom did you go?

Walking is a complete body exercise that gives fitness and increases the stamina. I am aware of it, but I have a **bad habit** of not going for a walk in the morning. My routine is busy and I have to rush for my classes but sometimes I go for an evening walk but it's not my routine. I remember my uncle came from Canada. He is a healthy man and enjoys healthy activities like going for walks, playing outdoor sports and having a balanced diet. I felt **motivated** by his healthy lifestyle. I remember last year he visited India and we went to Shimla. There, we had a long walk. He is a **knowledgeable man,** and during the walk we enjoyed the beautiful view of mountains and waterfall. There was no pollution and a fresh environment. I discussed **about my future plan.** He guided me about different courses, fee structure, colleges and rues of PR. He also advised me to improve my practical skills, remove hesitation and improve my art of communication for better settlement. It was **fruitful advice,** which helped me make the difficult decision of going abroad. After this walk, I had a change in my life. I planned to go to Canada for my better career and I was **motivated to change** my bad habit of not going for walks, because my uncle at the age of 70 goes for walks regularly and is perfectly healthy. So this was a memorable walk.

Questions

1. Bad habit

2. Healthy man

3. Motivation

4. Knowledgeable person

5. Future plan

6. Advice

7. Difficult decision

8. Change in my life

Cue Cards

- Talk about a bad habit you have.

    1. Why do you think it is bad?

    2. Are you planning to change it?

- Talk about an advice you receive

    1. What was it about

    2. Who guided you

    3. Why do you think it is useful?

- Talk about a person who enjoys healthy activities

    1. Who is he/she

    2. What activity do they enjoy?

    3. Are you motivated by them?

    4. What is the importance of good health?

- Talk about some motivation you received.

    1. What was it?

    2. Why were you motivated?

    3. How did it help you?

- Talk about a knowledgeable person you know

    1. Who is he/she?

    2. Why do you think they are knowledgeable?

    3. Talk about the benefit you received from that person.

- Talk about some advice you received for your future

  1. What was the advice?

  2. Who gave it to you?

  3. Was it beneficial?

- Talk about a difficult decision you made in your life.

  1. What was it?

  2. Who guided you to make the correct decision?

  3. Why did you trust that person?

- Talk about a change in your life.

  1. What was the change?

  2. Who motivated you to change?

  3. Is that change helping you develop your personality?

Note: **All the underlined words are cue cards. You can study and build ideas to make the cue cards by yourself.**

HANDICRAFT

Handicraft is a small-scale industry which generates self-employment and revenue in the society. It is the traditional skill and family business which is carried forward by the generations. Moreover, it is the regional art and craft which reflects culture and tradition. A handicraft, more precisely, is a type of work where useful and decorative objects are made completely by hand or using simple tools.

I live in Amritsar, and it is very famous for its phulkari. I remember I was assigned homework. It was a group **assignment.** We were five friends and we visited a nearby village. I was surprised to see the people of every age group busy making handicraft. They were doing embroidery on a piece of cloth. Colourful and attractive threads were used to decorate bed sheets. **I tried my best to learn a few stitches** but I could not get the perfection. It is a practical skill which can only be acquired over a period of time. Then, I made **a project report** in which I discussed the reasons for the downfall of this industry. Most of the people replied that **technology** makes the work very fast. So, they do not prefer using manual labour. Then, I provided a **solution;** handicraft should be preserved because it is a small-scale industry which is providing self-employment. Moreover, it reflects culture. This report was **appreciated** by my teachers and also by my seniors. My visit to this village was **the best learning experience** for me.

Questions

1. Assignment
2. Learn a new skill
3. Project report
4. Technology
5. Solution
6. Appreciation
7. Learning experience

- Talk about an assignment or a project you had in your school.

    1. What was it?

    2. Were you able to complete?

    3. What was your experience?

- Talk about a new skill that you wish to learn in the future.

    1. What is it?

    2. Why do you want to learn it?

    3. How will it help you?

    4. What is the future of that skill?

- Talk about a project you made in your school.

    1. What was it?

    2. How has that project report influenced you?

    3. What are the benefits of making project reports?

- Talk about a traditional skill that is declining with the advent (coming) of technology.

    1. Why do think so?

    2. Share the experience?

    3. How can you preserve?

- Talk about a solution that you provided and were appreciated for.

    1. What was it?

    2. Who appreciated you?

    3. Why do think it is important?

- Talk about a practical learning experience you had.

    1. What was it?

    2. Why do you think it was learning?

    3. What observations you had while learning?

<u>Note:</u> All the underlined words are cue cards. You can study and build the ideas to make the cue cards by yourself.

<u>Writing task 2:</u> You can practice this task by reading the above notes. Question) With the advent of technical skills, traditional skills are falling down. Some people say it is pointless to preserve the traditional skills. Discuss the statement and give your opinion.

Hands-On

➤ Practice CUE CARDS

Q1. Talk about teaching something to someone.

    a. What was it that you taught?

    b. Was it difficult for you to teach/learn that thing?

    c. What is the best method to learn that thing?

Q2. Describe a popular book that you read.

    a. When did you read it?

    b. Did you like it? Why?

    c. Was it by a famous author?

    d. How did people react to it?

Q3. Describe a road trip that you clearly remember.

    a. Where did you go?

    b. What did you do?

    c. Why do you remember this trip?

Q4. Describe a popular person.

    a. Who is that person?

    b. What does he/she do?

    c. Why is he/she popular?

    d. Do you like him/her? Why/why not?

Q5. Describe a situation from when you threw a party.

    a. Why or what were you celebrating?

    b. Where did you throw it?

    c. Who all were invited?

    d. How often do you throw party?

Q6. Talk about a place you would like to visit with your friends.

    a. Where would you go?

    b. What activities would you perform?

    c. Where do you go with your friends usually?

Q7. Describe a time when you were happy to use your cell phone.

    a. What was the incident?

    b. When was it?

    c. Has it happened again after that?

Q8. Describe a place you can go to listen to music.

    a. Where is this place?

    b. How often do you go there?

    c. What do other people like to do there?

Q9. Describe an activity you perform to keep yourself healthy.

    a. How often do you do it?

    b. What are its other benefits?

    c. Is it a popular health activity?

    d. How do people in your society keep themselves healthy?

Q10. Talk about a creative person you admire.

    a. Who is this person?

    b. What does he/she do?

    c. Is he/she a popular personality in your country?

    d. Are creative people desired and respected in your society?

Still Confused?

Here are some tips and simple solutions to tense situations during the speaking test.

- If you could not understand the question of examiner.

  ➤ You have to ask the examiner to make it understandable by saying, "Sorry, I could not understand your question."

- If you could not hear the question.

  ➤ Say, "Pardon sir?"

- If you simply do not know the answer to the question.

  ➤ Say, "Sorry, sir."

- If you handle such situations cleverly, you will give the examiner the idea that you are prepared for the test and are not afraid of it.

DO'S

✓ Always quote an example when they ask you "WHY".

✓ Always try to paraphrase the question.

✓ E.g.: Q: What is your name? A: My name is …

✓ Always make notes on cue cards. It helps you with fluency and in building a thought process.

✓ Before entering the examination hall, talk to yourself in English and make yourself comfortable with the language before the actual test.

✓ Lastly, make sure you practice at least 15 minutes of speaking daily.

DON'TS

✗ Don't memorize your answers. It gives a negative impression.

✗ Don't give priority to grammar over fluency.

✗ Don't add "big" words if you do not know their meaning or can't make proper use of them.

✗ Don't worry about the examiner's point of view, he's not there to judge your thinking.

✗ Lastly, never be late for an interview. Be on time and well prepared.

Vocabulary

A

1. **Ambidextrous:** one who uses both hands equally well.

2. **Ambiance:** type or character of an atmosphere or place

3. **Anarchy:** absence of government

4. **Anonymous:** unknown

5. **Avaricious:** extremely desirous of money

6. **Abysmal:** extremely bad

7. **Annihilate:** destroy utterly

8. **Aberration:** a state or condition markedly different from the norm

9. **Adulation:** exaggerated flattery or praise

10. **Arbitrary:** based on or subject to individual discretion or preference

B

11. **Brittle:** hard but liable to be easily broken

12. **Banish:** send away from home or country as a form of punishment

13. **Bereavement:** death in family

14. **Barricade:** to block with barriers

15. **Brandish:** move or swing back and forth

C

16. **Commotion:** confused movement

17. **Concoction:** any foodstuff made by combining different ingredients

288

18. **Conspicuous:** obvious to the eye or mind

19. **Contortion:** a tortuous and twisted shape or position

20. **Cunning:** shrewdness as demonstrated by being skilled in deception

21. **Conundrum:** a confusing and difficult problem

D

22. **Debris:** the remains of something that has been destroyed

23. **Defiance:** a hostile challenge

24. **Deft:** skilful in physical movements; especially of the hands

25. **Disdain:** lack of respect accompanied by a feeling of intense dislike

26. **Dismal:** causing dejection

E

27. **Eavesdrop:** listen without the speaker's knowledge

28. **Egregious:** conspicuously and outrageously bad

29. **Engross:** consume all of one's attention or time

30. **Exasperation:** a feeling of annoyance

31. **Exhilarate:** fill with sublime emotion

F

32. **Falter:** move hesitatingly, as if about to give way

33. **Foresight:** seeing ahead; knowing in advance; foreseeing

34. **Furtive:** secret and sly or sordid

G

35. **Gruelling:** characterized by effort to the point of exhaustion

36. **Gusto:** vigorous and enthusiastic enjoyment

H

37. **Hasten:** speed up the progress of; facilitate

38. **Headway:** forward movement

39. **Hostile:** unfriendly

40. **Hinder:** to stop

41. **Hallucinations:** seeing imaginary things

I

42. **Ignite:** to cause to start burning

43. **Illuminate:** make free from confusion or ambiguity

44. **Impending:** close in time; about to occur

45. **Imperious:** having or showing arrogant superiority

46. **Imperative:** crucial; vital; important

J

47. **Jabber:** talk in a noisy, excited, or declamatory manner

48. **Jargon:** technical terminology characteristic of a particular subject

49. **Jostle:** make one's way by pushing or shoving

50. **Jut:** extend out or project in space

K

51. **Ken:** range of what one can know or understand

52. **Kindle:** call forth, as an emotion, feeling, or response

53. **Knoll:** a small natural hill

L

54. **Luminous:** softly bright or radiant

55. **Linguist:** one who knows many languages

56. **Loquacious:** a person fond of talking

57. **Lucid:** transparently clear; easily understandable

M

58. **Mercenary:** those who work only for money

59. **Melancholy:** a constitutional tendency to be gloomy and depressed

60. **Meander:** move or cause to move in a sinuous or circular course

61. **Mob:** a disorderly crowd of people

62. **Meticulous:** marked by extreme care in treatment of details

N

63. **Narrate:** give a detailed account of

64. **Notorious:** having a bad reputation

65. **Numb:** to lose senses/stop feeling anything

66. **Nostalgic:** unhappy about being away and longing for familiar things

67. **Negligence:** ignoring or lack of awareness

O

68. **Oxymoron:** conjoining contradictory terms

69. **Omnipresent:** someone who's present everywhere

70. **Optimistic:** someone who always sees the bright side of something

71. **Obscure:** not clearly understood or expressed

72. **Obsolete:** not used anymore

P

73. **Parasite:** an animal or person living on another

74. **Pertinent:** having precise or logical relevance to the matter at hand

75. **Persistent:** stubbornly unyielding

76. **Pristine:** completely free from dirt or contamination

77. **Pique:** a sudden outburst of anger

78. **Paradigm:** a standard or typical example

Q

79. **Quell:** overcome or allay

80. **Quixotic:** not sensible about practical matters

R

81. **Rambunctious:** noisy and lacking in restraint or discipline

82. **Rhetorical:** relating to using language effectively

83. **Recluse:** one who lives in solitude

84. **Recuperate:** restore to good health or strength

85. **Repugnant:** offensive to the mind

86. **Restitution:** a sum of money paid in compensation for loss

S

87. **Sabotage:** destroy property or hinder normal operations

88. **Scurry:** move about or proceed hurriedly

89. **Serenity:** the absence of mental stress or anxiety

90. **Sombre:** grave or even gloomy in character

91. **Spurious:** plausible but false

92. **Swarm:** move in large numbers

93. **Stupefy:** make dull or muddle, as with intoxication

94. **Serendipity:** good luck in making unexpected and fortunate discoveries

95. **Satiate:** fill to satisfaction

96. **Saccharine:** overly sweet

T

97. **Transient:** lasting a very short time

98. **Temerity:** fearless daring

99. **Tactic:** a plan for attaining a particular goal

100. **Tangible:** perceptible by the senses especially the sense of touch

U-Z

101. **Uncanny:** surpassing the ordinary or normal

102. **Versatile:** able to move freely in all directions

103. **Vigilant:** carefully observant or attentive

104. **Vulnerable:** capable of being wounded or hurt

105. **Zeal:** a feeling of strong eagerness

TEST YOURSELF IN WRITING

TEST 1

Academic Writing Task 1

The line graph below shows the number of annual visits to Australia by overseas residents. The table below gives information on the country of origin where the visitors came from. Write a report for a university lecturer describing the information given.

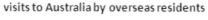

	1975	2005
SOUTH KOREA	2.9	9.1
JAPAN	3.2	12.0
CHINA	0.3	0.8
USA	0.4	1.1
BRITAIN	0.9	2.9
EUROPE	1.1	4.5
Total	8.8	30.4
NUMBER OF VISITORS (million)		

GENERAL WRITING TASK – 1

Q: Write a letter to your friend and recommend a good place that you have visited before for a holiday. Say where you went, where you stayed, what you can do there and what the food was like.

_____

_____

_____

_____

_____

_____

_____

_____

_____

_____

_____

_____

_____

_____

_____

_____

_____

_____

_____

_____

_____

_____

_____

WRITING TASK – 2

Do you agree or disagree with the following statement?

Parents are the best teachers. Use specific reasons and examples to support your answer.

_____

_____

_____

_____

_____

_____

_____

_____

_____

_____

_____

_____

_____

_____

_____

_____

_____

_____

_____

_____

_____

_____

_____

_____

_____

TEST 2

Academic Writing Task 1

The diagram shows the procedure for university entry for high school graduates.

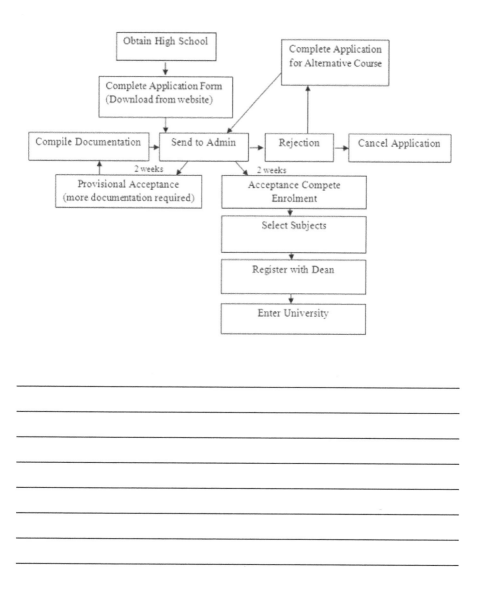

_____

_____

_____

_____

_____

_____

_____

_____

GENERAL WRITING TASK – 1

Your friend has just returned from the States. You cannot receive him/
her at the airport. Write a letter to him/her and clarify your position.

_____

_____

_____

_____

_____

_____

_____

_____

_____

_____

_____

_____

_____

_____

_____

_____

_____

_____

_____

_____

_____

_____

_____

_____

WRITING TASK – 2

These days, people are living to their 90s and beyond. As a result, there is increasing concern about care for the elderly.

Do you think it is the responsibility of the family to care for their elderly members or should the government be held responsible?

_____

_____

_____

_____

_____

_____

_____

_____

_____

_____

_____

_____

_____

_____

_____

_____

_____

_____

_____

_____

_____

_____

TEST 3

Academic Writing Task 1

The following diagram shows how greenhouse gases trap energy from the Sun.

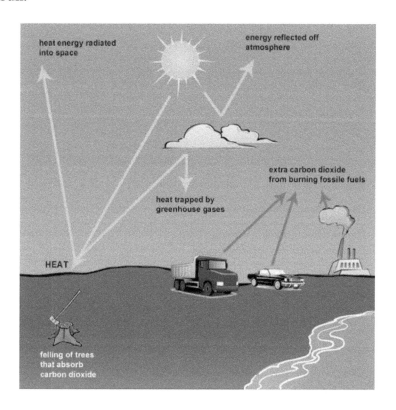

GENERAL WRITING TASK – 1

While travelling by metro, your credit card slipped out of your pocket. You realized this only after reaching home. Write a letter to the concerned authorities and explain what happened.

_____

_____

_____

_____

_____

_____

_____

_____

_____

_____

_____

_____

_____

_____

_____

_____

_____

_____

_____

_____

_____

_____

_____

_____

WRITING TASK – 2

We are seeing a significant increase in online shopping today. What are the advantages and disadvantages of this trend? Give your opinion and relevant examples.

_____

_____

_____

_____

_____

_____

_____

_____

_____

_____

_____

_____

_____

_____

_____

_____

_____

_____

_____

_____

_____

_____

_____

TEST 4

ACADEMIC WRITING TASK 1

The table below gives information about Favourite Pastimes in different countries.

	From 30–50 Years Old						
	TV	Sport	Reading	Hobbies	Music	Beach	Sleep
Canada	60	22	15	40	3	0	2
France	/	/	30	20	4	/	/
England	/	/	30	21	4	/	20
Australia	65	30	15	45	5	30	4
Korea	22	21	60	45	2	2	4
China	15	25	60	50	0	5	5
USA	60	23	15	42	23	30	2
Japan	/	/	62	/	/	/	/

GENERAL WRITING TASK – 1

You travelled by plane last week and your luggage was lost. You have still heard nothing from the airline company.

Write to the airline explaining what happened. Describe your luggage and tell them what was in it. Find out what they are going to do about it.

_____

_____

_____

_____

_____

_____

_____

_____

_____

_____

_____

_____

_____

_____

_____

_____

_____

_____

_____

_____

_____

_____

WRITING TASK – 2

Some people think that humans can use animals in any way for their own benefit. Others, however, believe that people should not use animals in the wrong way. Discuss both these views and give your own opinion.

_____

_____

_____

_____

_____

_____

_____

_____

_____

_____

_____

_____

_____

_____

_____

_____

_____

_____

_____

The contents of this book have been designed after comprehensive research from various online forums and, based on the experience of the author, the best has been extracted. Reference links have been provided below for further guidance and assistance for the students.

http://sckool.org/ielts-reading-test.html?page=9

https://ielts-up.com/reading/academic-reading-sample-8.1.html

https://ielts-mentor.com/reading-sample/gt-reading/3135-renting-accommodation-in-stonington-and-blossom-child-care

https://www.ielts-mentor.com/reading-sample/gt-reading/3185-shoe-world-and-cd-directory

ahaniwal @ unionbank of India. com.

ph n-